WORLD BIBLE NEWS PROPHECY

C. J. Neff

20105 NE Kings Grade Rd.

Newberg, Oregon 97132

"Focusing attention on Israel, the Middle East, and Europe, this work is both sane and sound. It will enlighten the mind, move the heart to love of the Lord, and motivate to a life pleasing to Him."

> *J. Dwight Pentecost, Distinguished Professor of Bible Exposition Emeritus, Dallas Theological Seminary*

"This well-written book shows how modern events relate to the prophecies of the Bible. Dr. Dyer's informative and inspirational style will challenge readers to live more for the next world than for this one."

> *Tim LaHaye, President*
> *Family Life Ministries*

"In forceful and frequently entertaining language, Dr. Charles Dyer brings current events into sharp focus in the light of Bible prophecy. Thoroughly conservative, the book appeals to readers to study the 'sure word of prophecy' and, like the prophets of old, to walk with God by faith."

> *Gerald B. Stanton, President*
> *Ambassadors International*

"Good prophecy. Good history. Good theology. Good writing. Good reading."

> *Charles C. Ryrie, Professor Emeritus*
> *Dallas Theological Seminary*

"The message of world news and Bible prophecy couldn't be more relevant. It's time for Christians to realize that they're going to stand before a holy God and give an account for the way they've lived. This book will open our eyes, help us align our thinking to God's infallible Word, and motivate us to live more responsibly."

> *Kay Arthur, Executive Vice President*
> *Precept Ministries*

WORLD NEWS AND BIBLE PROPHECY

CHARLES H. DYER

TYNDALE HOUSE PUBLISHERS
WHEATON, ILLINOIS

The *"NIV"* and *"New International Version"* trademarks are registered in
the United States Patent and Trademark Office by International Bible
Society. Use of either trademark requires the permission of International
Bible Society.

Unless otherwise noted, Scripture quotations are taken from the *Holy
Bible,* New International Version®, copyright © 1973, 1978, 1984 by Inter-
national Bible Society. Used by permission of Zondervan Publishing
House. All rights reserved.

Scripture quotations marked KJV are taken from the *Holy Bible,* King
James Version.

Library of Congress Cataloging-in-Publication Data

Dyer, Charles H., date
  World news and Bible prophecy / Charles H. Dyer.
    p. cm.
  Includes index.
  ISBN 0-8423-5017-9 ISBN 0-8423-5019-5, foreign
  1. Bible—Prophecies. 2. Eschatology. 3. World
politics—1985-1995. I. Title.
BS647.2.D94 1993
220.1'5—dc20   92-42522

Printed in the United States of America

99 98 97 96 95 94 93
9   8   7   6   5   4   3   2

This book is dedicated to several teachers and mentors who have made a profound impact on my life and ministry:

WILLIS BISHOP
who kindled in me a love for the Old Testament and for the people of Israel

HARRY FLETCHER
who modeled for me the life of a godly leader

HOWARD HENDRICKS
who motivated me to move God's truth from my head to my heart

PAUL MANGUM
who encouraged me to follow my convictions

JIM SCHUPPE
who showed me how to study the Bible

JOHN WALVOORD
who imparted to me a love for eschatology

> *But as for you,*
> *continue in what you have learned*
> *and have become convinced of,*
> *because you know those*
> *from whom you learned it.*
>   2 TIMOTHY 3:14

CONTENTS

FOREWORD

In the Gospel of Matthew 16:1-4, Christ rebuked the
Pharisees for their blindness to the signs of the times.
Before their eyes Christ was performing the predicted
evidences that He was indeed the Messiah.

In the modern scene, religious leaders, generally
speaking, are following the same pattern of being
blind to the things that are happening in the world that
are related to the prophetic program of God. Much of
this is due to their unbelief and their lack of knowledge about what the Bible actually teaches.

In the subject of signs of the Lord's return, clear
thinking is involved. The Rapture of the church, which
is the next event, has no signs. What we are seeing in
the world today are signs of approaching events that
will follow the Rapture. Some of these are major, like
the movement toward a world government, a concentration on Middle East problems, and modern technology that makes possible a world government predicted
for the end times. Opinions may vary as to the significance of other lesser signs, but the main point is made
clear. While no time schedule is justified from Scrip-

ture, the fact that the coming of the Lord in the air may be very near is recognized even by some secular sources.

This volume is a penetrating study of the many evidences that relate Bible prophecy to world news. Readers may not agree with every detail, but the main conclusion is clear enough. World news is significant as related to prophetic truths. This should alert the people of God to the urgency of the gospel task and to the necessity of living expectantly for that great moment when the shout will come from the blue and the church will be on its way to Glory. Readers will find this book packed with facts and details that relate our present world to biblical prophecy, all welded together in a great picture of end-time events.

John F. Walvoord
Chancellor, Dallas Theological Seminary
Author, *Armageddon, Oil & the Middle East Crisis*

INTRODUCTION: THE DAWNING OF A NEW MILLENNIUM

Chicago, November 27, 1991. The Doomsday Clock, on the cover of the *Bulletin of the Atomic Scientists,* was turned back to 11:43 P.M.—its farthest point ever from "nuclear midnight." An accompanying editorial explained the reason for this optimistic change. "The Cold War is over. The 40-year-long East-West nuclear arms race has ended."[1]

> But it is not too early to begin reflecting about the nature of a new world order in conditions that now seem quite foreseeable. . . . And if the moment is seized, it could mark a historic watershed when the attention of the world turned decisively towards creating a lasting structure of peace.—Henry Kissinger, following the failed coup attempt in the Soviet Union[2]

> While people are saying, "Peace and safety," destruction will come on them suddenly, as labor pains on a pregnant woman, and they will not escape. (1 Thessalonians 5:3)

The world races toward the year 2000 and the dawning of a new millennium. What surprises await us? Will the coming years bring world peace and prosperity, or will they produce decades of despair? Optimists point to the collapse of Communism, the thawing of the Cold War, and the release of American hostages in the Middle East as hopeful hints of what the future holds. Pessimists watch rising ethnic violence, growing environmental threats, a widening gap between the "have" and "have-not" nations, and the proliferation of nuclear technology and see a recipe for global disaster.

Can anyone predict the future? From the stock market to Eastern Europe and the Middle East, experts have tried to discern what the future holds. And most have not done well! In the early 1980s the United States began the largest peacetime military buildup in history. Their goal was to counter the threat of the "evil empire"—the Communist colossus called the Soviet Union. No one at the time predicted the quick collapse of Eastern Europe or the Soviet Union. In 1987 the United States, Western Europe, Saudi Arabia, and Kuwait were working quietly to help Saddam Hussein shore up his military machine. Who predicted that within three years he would invade Kuwait and force the world to respond to his aggression? Such obvious blunders in anticipating world events left even the experts dumbfounded. Can we discern the future, or are all attempts doomed to failure?

World history has never been kind to those who claim to know the future. But amidst the wreckage of failed forecasts stands one notable exception. The Bible! In the Bible God claims to predict the future. More than 25 percent of the Bible, when written, predicted events before they occurred. And God's "batting average" is remarkable—He has never been wrong! Through the centuries history has proven the absolute accuracy of God's predictions of the future. Since God knows the end from the beginning (and since He is in control of the universe), only He can accurately foretell future events.

Crystal Ball or Kaleidoscope?

God's Word might predict the future, but that is of little help to those who cannot make heads or tails of the Bible. While some view the Bible as a cosmic crystal ball with secrets available to those who peer into its pages, others read the same Scriptures and see only a kaleidoscope of images and visions that make no apparent sense. Does the Bible present a plan for the ages, or is it just a collection of disconnected books written at various times to various people?

God declared that He was the author of the Bible and its prophecies. "Above all, you must understand that no prophecy of Scripture came about by the prophet's own interpretation. For prophecy never had its origin in the will of man, but men spoke from God as they were carried along by the Holy Spirit" (2 Peter 1:20-21). God is the ultimate Author of the Bible, and He did not stutter when He spoke.

Reading today's newspaper is like looking at a table covered with pieces of a jigsaw puzzle. Each article is interesting, but it remains disconnected from the articles that surround it. The key to putting together a jigsaw puzzle is to use the picture on the box as your guide. By following the picture you can look at each puzzle piece and determine where it fits in the overall plan. In the same way, by understanding the master plan of God's Word you can evaluate the many events in the world and see how they fit together in God's program for history.

Unscrambling an Egg

Many people are afraid to study the prophecies of the Bible because they believe they are incapable of understanding them. The way many well-intentioned preachers and scholars use the Bible does not help the self-confidence of the average reader. They cite obscure verses from unfamiliar books of the Bible as clear revelations from God on current events. Those bold enough to look up the verses find references to names and places they have never heard before. Quietly they close their Bibles and nod their heads as though they actually understand the allusions to names they can not even pronounce. Convinced that the "average person" has no more chance of understanding the Bible than of unscrambling an egg, they quit trying.

But God did not intend for His Word to be as incomprehensible to the average person as a book on nuclear physics written in another language. God gave the Bible—including Bible prophecy—for "normal" people, and it can be understood by the average person today. In this book I will look at key events in God's prophetic Word and explain what the Bible says about those events. Along the way I also will illustrate those prophecies with current world events.

I have divided the book into four sections. The first section focuses on Israel's role in end-time events. God's program for Israel is at the heart of His plans for the world. The second section explores the role of other Middle Eastern countries—Russia, Turkey, Iran, and Iraq—in Bible prophecy. What place do oil and the Islamic religion play in God's prophetic drama? The third section examines Europe's role in prophecy. Will Europe unite? And if it does, how will this New

World Order affect the Middle East and the rest of the world?

The fourth section of the book moves from the future to the present. How do tomorrow's headlines meet today's needs? Can we be sure God really did predict the future? If he did, what practical benefit does it have for us today?

Bear in mind that events today are not yet the fulfillment of Bible prophecy. As I wrote in *The Rise of Babylon,* the curtain has not yet risen on the final act of God's drama for this present age. The houselights have not yet dimmed, but we can still perceive activity taking place behind the curtain. God is arranging the scenery in its proper place and is allowing the actors to assume their positions on the world stage. When everything is in order, God will allow the curtain to go up.

As we look at and evaluate current world events, we want to understand what role they might be playing to set the stage for the events prophesied in the Bible. At the same time we must remember that, as the world continues to change, only God knows the future. We must evaluate current events in light of the Bible, and not the other way around. We need to know and understand Bible prophecy so that we can more wisely discern the role of current world events.

So let's take our seats, grab our Bibles, and see what God has in store for tomorrow's newspaper.

PART ONE

ISRAEL: IN THE EYE OF THE HURRICANE

Sunlight squeezed past the buildings guarding each side of the narrow street and settled in puddles of brightness on the limestone paving below. The street, well worn from countless sandals and shoes, snaked its way through these patches of light on its way to the Damascus Gate. Visitors to Israel wind their way through this maze of streets and alleys as the sights, sounds, and smells of Jerusalem transport them back in time. Merchants and vendors—as if from the pages of the Bible—hawking everything from olive-wood camels to shish kabob, cry out to those passing by.

But this morning something was amiss. Instead of unpacking their wares and opening for business, I saw vendors and merchants hastily shuttering their shops and vanishing into doorways and alleys. The Arab uprising, or Intifada, against Israel often turned into a war of graffiti and symbolic strikes, but today was not a strike day. My students followed close behind me as the street twisted to the left, and in the distance we saw the cause for this sudden shutdown.

Two groups stood facing each other, barely fifty feet apart. Those closest to us held an Israeli flag fluttering from a pole. Those in the distance wrapped their heads in kaffiyehs—black-and-white checkered head coverings identifying them as supporters of the PLO. Though the groups shouted at one another in Arabic and Hebrew, the expressions on their faces left no doubt about the exact meaning of their words.

I stood entranced, watching a bizarre ballet unfold on the narrow stage before me. Would rocks and stones soon follow the slogans being hurled by the mob? I decided we would not wait around to find out.

Ducking into a side street, we wound our way around the conflict. A short distance away we turned onto a parallel street that would take us to the Damascus Gate. Shoppers crowded the street, and merchants sat in the doorways of their shops urging us to step inside and bargain for their baubles. A three-minute walk from confrontation to commerce! But even more remarkable was the fact that, after three weeks in Israel, this all seemed so perfectly normal.

Israel. The modern nation has yet to celebrate its fiftieth birthday, yet it commands center stage in world events. The struggle over Israel's right to exist as a nation has affected the world in far greater measure than one would expect given its size, population, or natural resources. The 1972 Olympic Games in Munich riveted the eyes of the world on Arab terrorists holding hostage —and then murdering—members of the Israeli Olympic Team. The world waited in gas lines in 1973 because of the Israeli-Arab Yom Kippur War. In 1991 Saddam Hussein tried to shatter the solidarity of the UN coalition against Iraq by launching Scud missles against Tel Aviv. Why does Israel play such a strategic role in world affairs?

Some search for secret conspiracies, with Jewish bankers and power brokers controlling the world. Such unfounded speculation appeals to anti-Semitic prejudice. From Russian pogroms to Hitler's "final solution" to criticism of America's "Zionist-controlled media," the world has not lacked individuals who blame their problems on the Jews. But Israel's strategic importance in the world today is not the result of some hidden plot devised by a small group of wealthy

Jews in a smoke-filled boardroom. I say this for two reasons. First, no such group exists. Second, the answer is much more profound—and biblical!

Israel stands at the center of the world stage because the Jews are God's chosen people. God selected Israel to play a pivotal role in world history. As the events of the world change with hurricane force, Israel will remain at the center—in the eye of the hurricane.

God gave Israel a starring role in His drama of the ages, and Israel will again take center stage in the final act. You cannot understand the future without understanding the part assigned to Israel. Much like the popular series of movies, we must go *Back to the Future* if we want to fit the pieces of God's prophetic puzzle together. Our starting place for the future begins when God "signed an agreement" with Abraham. Let's join the signing ceremony already in progress.

CHAPTER ONE
BACK TO THE FUTURE

Bible teachers often call the book of Genesis the "Book of Beginnings," but the first eleven chapters could more aptly be described as a book of human bunglings. These chapters do not paint an optimistic picture of humanity's early history. Adam and Eve disobeyed God and marred the perfection of God's creation. Because of their sin, God expelled them from the Garden of Eden. Sin—a disease of the soul transmitted from those first ancestors—separated humanity from God. The human race excelled in evil and reached a point where God had to judge the world. Only Noah and his family survived the flood that destroyed the earth. God started anew with Noah and his descendants, but they still possessed the sin nature that they inherited from Adam. God's grand new plan for humanity was buried beneath the bricks and bitumen at the Tower of Babel. Again the human race showed its unwillingness to follow God.

God responded by turning the Tower of Babel into a tumult of confusion. By creating multiple languages, God forced humanity to stop building. Families joined with other families who spoke the same language, and the different people groups went their separate ways. Anyone who, as an adult, has tried to master another language knows how effective God's plan was! But the division of humanity by language caused another problem. How could God reach these new nations and unite them again in His plans for blessing?

Abraham Believed God

God's solution was to choose one man who, with his descendants, would serve as God's "missionary" to the rest of the world. God selected Abraham and made him an offer he couldn't refuse.

> I will make you into a great nation and I will bless you; I will make your name great, and you will be a blessing. I will bless those who bless you, and whoever curses you I will curse; and all peoples on earth will be blessed through you. (Genesis 12:2-3)

Abraham, originally called Abram, didn't fully understand all the details of God's plan, but he obeyed God. Leaving family and friends, he traveled to a new land. Being in the will of God did not exempt Abram from difficulties. He struggled with famine, family problems, foreign invaders, and a faith in God that wavered at times (Genesis 12–14). Yet he believed the promise God had made.

Genesis 15 exposes Abram's brief struggle with mid-life crisis—at the age of eighty-five! God promised to make Abram into a "great nation" when He called him. Abram was seventy-five years old at the time (12:4), and his wife was sixty-five. He was more than willing to start a family, but his wife was infertile and had been unable to bear children throughout their marriage (11:30). Undoubtedly Abram believed God would do a miracle in Sarai's life to make her fertile. But by the time Genesis 15 rolled around, ten years had elapsed—and by that time Sarai (later Sarah) had gone through menopause.

Abram's frustration appears early in Genesis 15 when he answers God's words of encouragement with a challenge. "O Sovereign LORD, what can you give me since I remain childless and the one who will inherit my estate is Eliezer of Damascus? . . . You have given me no children; so a servant in my household will be my heir" (15:2-3). Ten long years of waiting had passed, and God's promise seemed more remote than ever.

God's answer to Abram boggles the mind. "This man [the servant Eliezer] will not be your heir, but a son coming from your own body will be your heir. . . . Look up at the heavens and count the stars—if indeed you can count them. . . . So shall your offspring be" (15:4-5). Get out the diapers, Abram; the babies will soon be born!

Abram's response—and God's reaction—is profound. "Abram believed the LORD, and he credited it to him as righteousness" (15:6). In spite of outward circumstances Abram believed in the promises of God. And it was his faith in God's promises that brought him into a right relationship with God. What made Abram righteous? Not his works. Not his wealth. Not his offerings. God declared Abram righteous because he chose to accept and trust what God had spoken.

Let's Make a Deal

A man struggling with faith once cried to Jesus, "I do believe; help me overcome my unbelief!" (Mark 9:24). I don't know about you, but that confusing cry epitomizes the struggles I have faced in my spiritual journey. I do believe God, and yet I still struggle with doubts about the depth or sincerity of my faith. I believe and I want to trust God even more—but I'm afraid to step out in faith.

Just like us, Abram also struggled. He wrestled with his doubts, but his faith finally triumphed. And yet, how could he reconcile his faith in God's promises with his circumstances? God promised him the land in which he lived (see Genesis 13:14-17), but foreign powers laid claim to more of the land than Abram ever owned. God promised him offspring (15:4-5), but his wife was an infertile woman past childbearing age. Abram needed God's reassurance that He could be trusted in spite of circumstances. So God wrote up a contract and "signed on the bottom line."

The world is obsessed with establishing contracts and agreements. Archaeologists have unearthed written contracts dating back to the time of Abram. God reassured Abram of the reliability of His promises by formalizing them as a covenant, a legally binding contract. The specifics sound bizarre to us today, but the last part of Genesis 15 describes the "signing cere-

mony" for this agreement. After killing and dividing
in half several animals, the partners in a contract
would walk together between the pieces of the animals. By doing so they were saying to each other,
"May you do this to me [kill me and cut me apart] if I
fail to keep my part of the agreement." People thought
twice before signing such an agreement!

After killing and dividing the animals, Abram fell
into a deep sleep (15:9-17). He awakened after dark as
"a smoking firepot with a blazing torch appeared and
passed between the pieces." Three observations are
crucial. First, Abram did not walk between the animals. God did not put Abram under any legal obligation in this contract. Second, the firepot and torch
represented God. God often manifested His visible
presence by using fire and smoke—from the burning
bush before Moses (Exodus 3:2) to the fire and smoke
on Mount Sinai (Exodus 19:18) to the cloud by day
and pillar of fire by night that went with Israel in the
wilderness (Numbers 9:15-16). Third, God and God
alone passed between the animals. A contract was
made, but God alone signed on the bottom line. God
pledged by His very life to keep His agreement with
Abram.

But what did God agree to do? "To your descendants I give this land" (Genesis 15:18). God vowed
that Abram would have descendants and that those
descendants would possess the land. Abram's real children would possess the real land of Israel. God guaran-
teed this with His life.

How significant is this covenant? It is foundational
to the rest of the Bible. More than 1,300 years later the

prophet Micah used it as proof that the nation of Israel would ultimately experience both physical and spiritual restoration. In Micah 7 the prophet pictures a still-future time when the nation will experience physical restoration: "The day for building your walls will come, the day for extending your boundaries" (7:11). The buildings will again go up, and the borders will be expanded. But Israel's urban renewal will be accompanied by spiritual renewal. "You will again have compassion on us; you will tread our sins underfoot and hurl all our iniquities into the depths of the sea" (7:19). How could Micah be so sure that God would restore the nation of Israel both physically and spiritually? Because God made a promise to Abraham! "You will be true to Jacob, and show mercy to Abraham, as you pledged on oath to our fathers in days long ago" (7:20). Micah could rely on it because God had made a promise.

Nearly 800 years later the writer of the book of Hebrews drew the same conclusion from God's oath to Abraham.

> When God made his promise to Abraham, since there was no one greater for him to swear by, he swore by himself, saying, "I will surely bless you and give you many descendants." . . . Men swear by someone greater than themselves, and the oath confirms what is said and puts an end to all argument. Because God wanted to make the unchanging nature of his purpose very clear to the heirs of what was promised, he confirmed it with an oath. (Hebrews 6:13-17)

God made a promise to Abraham and his descendants, and He intends to keep it.

The Blessings and Cursings

If God promised Abraham and his descendants the land of Israel, how come the nation seems to spend more time out of the land than in it? The answer can be found in another agreement made between God and the nation of Israel at the time of Moses. If Abraham and the other patriarchs were the seed from which the nation of Israel was ultimately born, the land of Egypt was the womb in which the nation grew until the time of birth. A small band of seventy who entered Egypt multiplied for 400 years until they became the mighty multitude who came out under the leadership of Moses.

This ragtag collection of tribes numbered nearly 2.5 million individuals, but they were not functioning as a nation. At Mount Sinai God gave the new nation its constitution and bylaws, found in the books of Exodus, Leviticus, and part of Numbers. Forty years later God repeated His commands and provided some additions to reflect the changing conditions of the new generation about to enter the land of promise. This "revised edition" of the Law is the book of Deuteronomy.

During both periods when God gave the Law to the people, He functioned in the role of a good parent. Having explained the standards of righteous conduct He expected from His people, God gave a series of "blessings" or rewards that He would give for obedience. He also outlined the "cursings" or punishments that would follow for disobedience. In His first giving of the Law, God described the blessings and cursings in Leviticus 26. In the second giving of the Law, God explained the blessings and cursings in Deuteronomy 28.

In both chapters the punishments mount if the people refuse to change their wrongful conduct. The final punishment is God's ultimate penalty to Israel for disobedience—temporary expulsion from the very land they were about to enter to possess. "I will scatter you among the nations and will draw out my sword and pursue you. Your land will be laid waste, and your cities will lie in ruins" (Leviticus 26:33). "You will be uprooted from the land you are entering to possess. Then the LORD will scatter you among all nations, from one end of the earth to the other" (Deuteronomy 28:63-64).

Yet, even when God imposed the "ultimate penalty," He still refused to give up completely on the people of Israel. In Leviticus 26 God announces in advance that He will wait for the nation to acknowledge its sin. Once it does, He says, "I will remember my covenant with Jacob and my covenant with Isaac and my covenant with Abraham, and I will remember the land. . . . I will not reject them or abhor them so as to destroy them completely, breaking my covenant with them. I am the LORD their God" (Leviticus 26:42, 44). Forty years later God made the same announcement. Even in captivity, if Israel will turn to God, "then the LORD your God will restore your fortunes and have compassion on you and gather you

again from all the nations where he scattered you"
(Deuteronomy 30:3).

God's contract with Abraham might be old and
worn, but it's still valid. An ancient king summoned
Balaam, a soothsayer, to curse the nation of Israel in
its infancy. As he climbed to the craggy heights overlooking the spot where Israel was camped, his host
hoped that he would call down the wrath of God on
the Israelites. Balaam's response shocked the king
who had called him: "God is not a man, that he should
lie, nor a son of man, that he should change his mind.
Does he speak and then not act? Does he promise and
not fulfill? I have received a command to bless; he has
blessed, and I cannot change it" (Numbers 23:19-20).
God promised Abraham and his descendants the land
of Israel, and God never breaks His promises. But
have these promises already been fulfilled, or does
Israel still have a future hope?

CHAPTER TWO
PROMISES, PROMISES

God's great promises to Abraham never came to pass in Abraham's day. God promised Abraham descendants as numerous as the stars of heaven. But Abraham only witnessed the birth of one "star" to his wife Sarah—his son Isaac. God promised the land of Canaan, but the only ground Abraham ever possessed was a burial plot for his wife and himself. The writer of the book of Hebrews notes this fact as he applauds the great faith of Abraham and Sarah: "All these people were still living by faith when they died. They did not receive the things promised; they only saw them and welcomed them from a distance" (Hebrews 11:13).

But Abraham's descendants did grow into a nation and possess the land of Israel. By the time of David and Solomon, Israel had grown into a power that possessed the land God had promised (1 Kings 4:20-21). And this raises an interesting question. Was God's covenant with Abraham a terminal contract or a perpetual contract? That is, once God enabled Israel to grow into a nation and to possess the land, had He discharged His part of the agreement, or did His obligation continue?

Let me illustrate the difference. An elderly widow went to talk with her oldest son. He was a successful businessman managing a large corporation. His climb up the corporate ladder had brought great joy to his mother. But his younger brother was not so fortunate. Born mildly retarded, he still lived at home with his aging mother. And she worried about his future. Who would take care of him after she died? She raised this issue with her oldest son. "Don't worry, Mom," the older son said. "I'll provide him with a job and a home." But the woman persisted. "I know you will help him initially, but once I'm gone will you continue to look out for him to see that his needs are met?" Is the son agreeing to a onetime act of kindness, or is he committing to a long-term obligation? To everyone involved the distinction is crucial.

Had God discharged His obligation to Abraham once He brought the nation into the land and enabled them to establish control? Or does the Abrahamic covenant commit God to a long-term relationship with the nation of Israel? The Bible suggests that the contract did not end once Israel as a nation possessed the land.

First, God's purpose in calling Abraham and giving him the land went beyond just events up to the time of David and Solomon. God's larger purpose in choosing Abraham and his descendants was to bless all nations: "All peoples on earth will be blessed through you" (Genesis 12:3). God's promise to bless the world remained unfulfilled at the time of David and Solomon.

Second, other Old Testament authors who wrote after the time of David and Solomon believed that God's agreement was still valid in their day. Micah the prophet wrote nearly three centuries after David and Solomon. But he based Israel's future physical and spiritual restoration on God's promise to Abraham, "as you pledged on oath to our fathers in days long ago" (Micah 7:20). The anonymous writer of Psalm 105 also realized that God's promise did not end with a given generation.

> He remembers his covenant forever, the word he commanded, for a thousand generations, the covenant he made with Abraham, the oath he swore to Isaac. He confirmed it to Jacob as a decree, to Israel as an everlasting covenant: "To you I will give the land of Canaan as the portion you will inherit." (Psalm 105:8-11)

The psalmist praises God for the enduring nature of His promise to Abraham—even after the time of David and Solomon.

Third, even the New Testament recognizes the enduring nature of God's covenant with Abraham. Before Jesus Christ was born, His mother recognized God's faithfulness to Israel through the child about to be born to her: "He has helped his servant Israel, remembering to be merciful to Abraham and his descendants forever, even as he said to our fathers" (Luke 1:54-55). God's promise to Abraham did not end when the nation possessed the land at the time of David and Solomon.

This Land Is Your Land

God promised Abraham land, but what are the specific boundaries? In Genesis 15:18, God stated the general boundaries: "To your descendants I give this land, from the river of Egypt to the great river, the Euphrates." From the Nile to the Euphrates! That's a large chunk of real estate and includes parts of what is today Egypt, Israel, Jordan, Iraq, Syria, and Lebanon. Does all this belong to Israel?

The answer is, probably not—for three reasons. First, God's boundaries are general, not specific. God told Abraham that the land He was giving him lay between the two great river civilizations of that day. The civilization of Egypt flourished along the Nile River, while the Mesopotamian civilizations dotted the banks of the Tigris and Euphrates rivers.

Second, God also defines the land promised to Abraham in terms of the people who lived there. Israel's land included "the land of the Kenites, Kenizzites, Kadmonites, Hittites, Perizzites, Rephaites, Amorites, Canaanites, Girgashites and Jebusites" (Genesis 15:19-21). From what we know historically, most of these groups lived in Israel proper (see Numbers 13:29; Joshua 11:1-3).

Third, God later gave very specific land boundaries; and these show the exact dimensions of the land promised to Israel. "Command the Israelites and say to them: 'When you enter Canaan, the land that will be allotted to you as an inheritance will have these boundaries'" (Numbers 34:2). God then traced Israel's borders from the Salt Sea (the modern Dead Sea) to the Wadi of Egypt (probably the Wadi el Arish in the Sinai peninsula) on the south (34:3-5). The western border was the Mediterranean Sea (called the Great Sea in 34:6). God's surveying line stretched along the north, incorporating most of what is today Lebanon and Syria (34:7-9). The eastern border looped down to the Sea of Galilee (called the Sea of Kinnereth) and went due south along the Jordan River and the Dead Sea (34:10-12). This is the specific land promised to Israel.

The prophet Ezekiel penned a remarkable but often overlooked passage describing the land promised to Israel. In the beginning of his book, he warned the people of Judah's coming collapse because of sin. However, the day news of Jerusalem's fall reached those in captivity, Ezekiel's message changed. From chapters 33 to 48, Ezekiel preached a message of hope. Israel and Judah would once again be restored to the land and experience the promised blessings of God.

Ezekiel patterns the final chapters of his book after the original exodus of Israel from Egypt. Just as in the time of Moses, God would again gather His chosen people and bring them to His Promised Land. But this time God would guarantee that everything would turn out better than it did during the first exodus. Ezekiel concluded chapter 39 by announcing God's intention to restore the nation. "I will now bring Jacob back from captivity and will have compassion on all the people of Israel, and I will be zealous for my holy name" (Ezekiel 39:25).

In the original exodus, after rescuing the Israelites from Egypt and leading them to Sinai, God established His relationship with the people by giving plans to build His tabernacle, where He could dwell among His people (Exodus 20–40). When the people finished building, "the glory of the LORD filled the tabernacle" (40:35). Ezekiel follows this pattern. After announcing that God would regather His people, Ezekiel provides plans for a new sanctuary, where God could dwell among His people (Ezekiel 40–43). His plans for this new temple are as detailed as those for the original tabernacle. After focusing on the building project, Ezekiel concluded his description by announcing, "The glory of the LORD filled the temple" (Ezekiel 43:5).

After sharing with Moses the plans for the tabernacle, God explained how the nation was to worship Him. The books of Leviticus and Numbers contain God's "operating instructions" for worship. Ezekiel follows the same pattern. After giving the architectural plans for the new temple, he then provides God's instructions for worship in this temple (43:13–44:31).

The book of Numbers ended with God's explanation of the land boundaries for Israel's first entrance into the land of promise. Ezekiel continues his parallel by restating God's land boundaries for this new entrance into the land. What is remarkable is that the land boundaries are identical. The land promised by God to Abraham and specified by God to Moses in Numbers 34 is the same land still promised to Israel after their destruction by Babylon. The specific boundaries did not change.

After entering the land for the first time, Joshua apportioned the land among the tribes (Joshua 14–21).

Ezekiel ends his book with a second apportioning of the land among the tribes (Ezekiel 48). The boundaries stay the same, but the specific areas assigned to the tribes will change.

God made an agreement with Abraham. Abraham's descendants, through his son Isaac, would be the nation chosen by God to bring His promised blessings to the rest of the world. God gave Abraham's descendants a permanent deed to a specific land. Generally described as the land between the Nile and the Euphrates, it was land that incorporated specific nations and had very specific boundaries. Present-day Israel includes much—but not all—of the land promised by God to Abraham's descendants. According to Ezekiel, the nation will some day possess it all. But when will all this happen?

CHAPTER THREE
THE NEW EXODUS

Zvi's parents fled from Germany just before the door of emigration slammed shut. In a modern-day exodus, making their way on foot, by car, and by boat, they arrived in Palestine in the late 1930s. The land was a dismal waste! Malaria and other diseases, fueled by coastal swamps and lack of sanitation, made life miserable. Hostile neighbors made life dangerous. Settling in the expanding community of Tel Aviv, Zvi's parents joined a growing number of immigrants who seized the opportunity to forge a new future in the land of their ancestors.

Though safe from the Holocaust consuming so many of their family in Europe, Zvi's parents still had to struggle for survival in their adopted land. The British soldiers who occupied Palestine were both protectors and persecutors. Jews fought alongside the British against the German threat from North Africa, but those same British soldiers often refused to help defend Jews from attack by their Arab neighbors. The thought of an independent State of Israel was a dim but growing hope in the hearts of Zvi's parents.

When the war ended, thousands of Jews who survived Hitler's death camps realized the enormity of their loss. They looked toward Palestine as a place of refuge and help. Thousands made the perilous journey only to be stopped from entering their land of promise by the British. Newly freed from concentration camps in Europe, they again found themselves behind barbed wire in British internment camps on the island of Cyprus.

During this period of turbulence and confusion, Zvi was born. He lived as a child in a city bustling with British patrols and secret Jewish groups working to oust the British and smuggle in Jews and weapons. Though too young to fight, Zvi witnessed the miraculous birth of the new State of Israel in May 1948. He also experienced the bitter struggle to keep Israel safe from attacking Arab armies. Today he points with pride at the broken remains of Israeli armored cars that litter the road from Tel Aviv to Jerusalem. To him they represent the heroism and sacrifice that gave birth to the modern State of Israel.

Israel today is a far cry from the feeble nation that struggled to survive those early years. A modern military powerhouse, Israel boasts the latest in armaments and weapons. Her growth and development seem almost miraculous. But is the rebirth and growth of the nation merely the result of Jewish energy and determination, or is it also the fulfillment of Bible prophecy?

A Valley of Dry Bones

Over twenty-five centuries ago another young Israeli sat among his fellow countrymen in Tel Aviv—but

this Tel Aviv was in Babylonia, not Israel.[1] His name
was Ezekiel, and he had been carried captive to Babylon as a young man of twenty-five. Nebuchadnezzar
brought Ezekiel and 10,000 other citizens of Judah
back to Babylon in 605 B.C. After five years in captivity, Ezekiel was summoned by God as a prophet to
God's people in the land of Babylon. His ministry
among the exiles was not easy, for the message God
asked him to deliver was one of impending doom and
judgment. The exiles were counting the days till they
would be allowed to return home to Jerusalem. Ezekiel informed them that they would not return to Jerusalem. Instead, Jerusalem would be destroyed, and its
few survivors would be coming to Babylon.

When Ezekiel began his prophecies of woe, God
took away his voice (Ezekiel 3:26-27). Ezekiel
became dumb—unable to speak unless he was giving
a message from God. Ezekiel's inability to talk was a
dramatic sign to the people of Israel, but it paled in
comparison to the later hardships he endured. On January 15, 588 B.C., the day the final siege of Jerusalem
began, God took away Ezekiel's wife (24:1-2, 15-27).
The untimely death of the woman described to Ezekiel by God as "the delight of your eyes" served as a
painful prelude to the sadness everyone in captivity
would feel when word reached them of Jerusalem's
fall.

Just under three years later, the captives in Tel Aviv
understood personally the sorrowful sign of the death
of Ezekiel's wife. On January 8, 585 B.C., the first
group of captives from Jerusalem arrived in Tel Aviv.
The Babylonians had broken through Jerusalem's

defenses on July 18, 586 B.C. (2 Kings 25:2-4). By August 14 all pockets of resistance had been quelled, and the search for everyone in hiding was complete. The city was secure. Babylon's commanders entered the city and began the process of destruction. The army systematically looted and then burned all the buildings of Jerusalem. The walls and all other defensive fortifications were dismantled, and everything of value was cataloged and carted away to Babylon.

The Babylonian soldiers captured those still alive in Jerusalem when the city fell. They carried the prisoners to Ramah, six miles north of Jerusalem, for processing. Those identified as leaders of the rebellion were executed immediately or taken to Nebuchadnezzar for final sentencing. Others were identified as likely candidates for slavery in Babylon and sent on the long march into captivity. The Babylonians freed the poor, the lame, and the elderly and allowed them to remain in Judah amidst the rubble.

The journey to Babylon was arduous and slow. Babylonian soldiers prodded the men, women, and children along on foot, while much of the booty rode on carts. The Jews in the remote villages of Babylon didn't hear about Jerusalem's fall till these new captives stumbled into town with the news. Thus on January 8, 585 B.C., almost six months after the city walls were breached, Ezekiel's fellow captives in Tel Aviv heard the news that confirmed the awful truth of Ezekiel's earlier messages: Jerusalem had fallen.

Yet the day that brought such sadness to the captives brought a new change in Ezekiel. "Now the evening before the man arrived, the hand of the LORD was upon me, and he opened my mouth before the man came to me in the morning. So my mouth was opened and I was no longer silent" (Ezekiel 33:22). Seven-and-a-half years of silence ended! As the captives mourned the loss of Jerusalem, God delivered a new series of messages to Ezekiel. These messages focused on the future restoration of Jerusalem.

Ezekiel's new message to Israel was as unbelievable to those sitting around in mourning as his earlier messages of judgment had been. The northern kingdom of Israel and the southern kingdom of Judah had now both gone into captivity. The city of Jerusalem was a heap of rubble. The temple of Solomon was in ruins. The last king from the line of David was bound in chains, rotting away in a Babylonian dungeon. All seemed lost, but Ezekiel began predicting the nation's coming restoration: "For I will take you out of the nations; I will gather you from all the countries and bring you back into your own land. . . . You will live in the land I gave your forefathers; you will be my people, and I will be your God" (36:24, 28).

But when would this restoration take place? How would Israel know when this fulfillment was complete? Ezekiel provides several clues in the immediate context. The passage would be fulfilled when Israel returned to the land both physically and spiritually:

> I will sprinkle clean water on you, and you will be clean; I will cleanse you from all your impurities and from all your idols. I will give you a new heart and put a new spirit in you; I will remove from you your heart of stone and give you a

> heart of flesh. And I will put my Spirit in you
> and move you to follow my decrees and be care-
> ful to keep my laws. (Ezekiel 36:25-27)

Lest his audience miss the connection between Israel's spiritual restoration and her physical restoration,
Ezekiel repeats the theme just a few verses later: "On
the day I cleanse you from all your sins, I will resettle
your towns, and the ruins will be rebuilt. The desolate
land will be cultivated instead of lying desolate in the
sight of all who pass through it" (36:33-34).

But how could this happen? How could Israel experience such a dramatic resurrection? The nation had
died the day Babylon smashed through the walls of
Jerusalem. Neither Nebuchadnezzar nor his descendants would ever allow the Jews to return to their
land. Could God possibly restore to life the nation of
Israel?

Ezekiel presented two graphic illustrations to drive
home the truth of his prophecy. In the first vision God
placed Ezekiel in the middle of a valley full of
bleached bones. After allowing Ezekiel to gaze on this
scene of desolation, God asked a profound question.
"Son of man, can these bones live?" (37:3). Can something that has died and deteriorated ever come back to
life? Ezekiel's response reflected a mixture of confidence in God and confusion. "I said, 'O Sovereign
LORD, you alone know'" (37:3). From a human perspective, something that has died cannot live again,
but with God all things are possible.

God commanded Ezekiel to prophesy to the bones,
and as he did they began to reassemble. In a parallel to

God's original creation of Adam, the bones and flesh appear and form into a body, and then "breath entered them; they came to life" (37:10). The word *breath* also can be translated "wind" or "spirit" and is the same word used in God's original creation of humanity. "The LORD God formed the man from the dust of the ground and breathed into his nostrils the breath of life, and the man became a living being" (Genesis 2:7).

Ezekiel pictures a new creation. Death reverts to life. But what is the point of his parable? God gives the interpretation beginning in Ezekiel 37:11. "These bones are the whole house of Israel." God is using the valley of dry bones to illustrate the message of chapter 36. Israel felt that they had died nationally. ("Our bones are dried up and our hope is gone; we are cut off.") The nation saw no hope for their restoration.

But just as Ezekiel watched the bones come together and God's breath of life enter them, so the nation of Israel would be restored and receive God's Holy Spirit. The bones joining and having flesh put back on symbolized God's restoration of the nation. He would bring Israel "back from the grave" nationally. "I am going to open your graves and bring you up from them; I will bring you back to the land of Israel" (37:12). The breath of life symbolized the Spirit that God promised would indwell the people as He restored them both physically and spiritually. "I will put my Spirit in you and you will live, and I will settle you in your own land" (37:14).

Ezekiel's first sign was a dramatic announcement that God can and will do the impossible in restoring His people physically and spiritually to the land. However, Ezekiel's second sign was just as dramatic. If the purpose for the first sign was to illustrate how God could restore the nation, the second sign was to show who would be included in this miraculous restoration.

Ezekiel took two sticks and wrote on them. On the first stick he wrote, "Belonging to Judah and the Israelites associated with him" (37:16). On the second stick he wrote, "Ephraim's stick, belonging to Joseph and all the house of Israel associated with him" (37:16). Ezekiel then bound the sticks together to form a single stick. You can almost hear his audience whispering, "Now what is that supposed to mean?"

The Mormons use this passage to show that the Bible predicted the *Book of Mormon.* After all, didn't the people of *Judah* write the Bible? And wasn't *Joseph* Smith the one whom God used to translate the *Book of Mormon?* And didn't God say to join the two sticks together? Unfortunately, many sincere people have fallen prey to such misuse of the Bible. Ezekiel's sign might be interpreted several ways unless God tells us what the sign means. But once God gives His interpretation of the sign, then any other interpretations must be rejected. God gives His interpretation immediately after the sign:

> I will take the Israelites out of the nations where
> they have gone. I will gather them from all
> around and bring them back into their own land.
> I will make them one nation in the land, on the
> mountains of Israel. There will be one king over
> all of them and they will never again be two

nations or be divided into two kingdoms. (Ezekiel 37:21-22)

Shortly after the death of Solomon in 930 B.C., the nation of Israel had divided in two. Ten tribes had rallied around a man from the tribe of Ephraim named Jeroboam and had formed the kingdom of Israel. Two tribes had remained loyal to Solomon's son Rehoboam and had formed the kingdom of Judah. These two kingdoms had endured times of cooperation and confrontation, but they had never reunited as a single nation. In 722 B.C. Assyria carried into captivity the northern kingdom of Israel. Less than 140 years later, Ezekiel recorded the destruction of the southern kingdom of Judah by Babylon.

Ezekiel's sign illustrated the extent of the restoration predicted by God. When the nation of Israel would be restored to the land, it would not be a partial homecoming. God promised that all Jews—those from both the northern and southern kingdoms—would return.

Two observations must be made. First, these predictions by Ezekiel have not yet been fulfilled. When the remnant returned to the land following the Babylonian captivity, not all the Jews returned. And those who did return did not experience national forgiveness of sin, the indwelling of the Holy Spirit, and the outpouring of God's blessing. You only need to read the books of Ezra, Nehemiah, Haggai, Zechariah, or Malachi to realize that those Jews who returned to the land struggled with the same problems faced by their ancestors.

Second, Ezekiel does not predict a "two-stage"

return in this passage. In the vision of the valley of dry bones, the bones first reform into a lifeless body, and then the Spirit enters the body to give life. Some have seen in this vision a two-part restoration of Israel—physical restoration to the land followed later by a spiritual restoration to God. Those who see a two-stage restoration see the first part fulfilled in 1948 when Israel became a nation. But is this what Ezekiel's vision is teaching?

Ezekiel's vision was illustrating the truth of Ezekiel 36, which predicted a physical *and* spiritual restoration of Israel. In Ezekiel 36 God gives no indication that the restoration is a two-step process. Also, in the vision of the dry bones, the two-step process occurs only in Ezekiel's description of the vision. The two phases are not described when God interprets the vision. In fact, God even reverses the steps in His interpretation: "I will put my Spirit in you and you will live, and I will settle you in your own land" (37:14). Ezekiel 37 does predict the restoration of the nation of Israel, but it does not specifically point to the 1948 restoration of the nation.

Next Year in Jerusalem

Seated around a table, feasting on roasted lamb and unleavened bread, each spring Jews reenact a ritual as old as the nation of Israel itself. As the youngest child asks the traditional questions, Jewish families remember their national deliverance from the bondage of Egypt. A chair sits empty, awaiting the arrival of Elijah, the prophet who is to come again before the appearance of the Messiah. As the meal closes, the thoughts of those gathered focus on the goal of Jewish nationalism. "Next year in Jerusalem!" The statement captures the heart of Zionism—the desire to recreate a new nation of Israel in the land and city promised by God to His people.

Scarcely had the last embers died out in war-ravaged Jerusalem when Jews began dreaming of the day they could return to rebuild their shattered city and nation. With the fall of the last Jewish outpost at Masada in A.D. 73, the Romans claimed to have crushed the rebellious nation. But the minting of the Judaea Capta coins was a bit premature. Less than seventy years had passed when Rome again had to send her forces back to Judah to quell the Bar Kokhba revolt.

Rome retaliated by wiping away all traces of Jewish influence and ownership. They renamed the capital city. From now on Jerusalem was to be called Aelia Capitolina. The new masters barred Jews from entering. Rome even stamped a new name on the land. The country of Judea was now to bear the name of the Philistines rather than that of the Jews—Palestine. But as the years went by, the power of Rome faded, while the hope of the Jews scattered around the world remained strong.

Jews entered the land and were driven from the land over the next 1,500 years. The prayer remained "Next year in Jerusalem," but no movement existed to make that desire a reality—until the end of the last century. A French journalist named Theodore Hertzl covered the trial of the French Jew Dreyfuss, and Hertzl saw clearly the hatred and anti-Semitic feelings lying under the surface of "modern" Europe. Hertzl

launched a crusade to promote the cause of Zionism—
the formation of a national homeland for the Jewish
people.

The group explored many countries—from Kenya
to Australia—but everyone kept coming back to the
land God had promised to Israel. The trickle of Jews
going back to Israel became a flood following the formation of the State of Israel in 1948. After almost
2,000 years, the Jews again had a national homeland.
However, not all was rosy.

For Jews, the State of Israel was an island of hope
surrounded by a sea of hostility. When the United
Nations voted to create the State of Israel, the land of
Palestine contained approximately 600,000 Jews and
1.2 million Arabs. And the nations on all sides
opposed the State of Israel. Still, European Jews who
survived the Nazi Holocaust and Sephardic Jews from
the slums of Baghdad made their way to this beacon
of freedom. By the 1960s the Jewish population of
Israel was well over 2 million.

Israel's mystique and sense of manifest destiny
reached its zenith in the Six-Day War of 1967. In the
time God took to create the universe, Israel captured
large portions of the ancient land of Israel from her
Arab neighbors. But in that moment of military triumph, Israel also sowed the seeds of internal anguish
and dissent because the captured land came complete
with a large Arab population. But Israel's Jewish population continued to increase.

The 1960s saw Israel emerge as the dominant military power in the Middle East. But the 1973 Yom
Kippur War shattered the myth of Israeli invulnerabil-

ity. Egypt and Syria launched a surprise attack against Israeli forces on two fronts. For several days the fate of Israel seemed to hang in the balance. Israel emerged victorious, but only after suffering horrific casualties and having her psyche damaged by being caught flat-footed in a surprise attack that came too close to succeeding.

As the 1970s merged into the 1980s, Israel entered a state of lethargy. Israel had won the wars, but the "cold war" that still raged on every border put economic and emotional strains on the country. In 1982 Israel lashed out by invading Lebanon—and endured her own version of Vietnam. Fighting a battle of attrition without well-defined goals and objectives, and watching public support at home and abroad evaporate, Israel emerged from Lebanon bruised and battered. Hyperinflation wracked the economy, and the political system lacked a strong leader to galvanize the country. Immigration slowed to a trickle as the Zionist dream became a nightmare. More Jews were emigrating from Israel than were moving to Israel.

But some Jews did want to return to Israel. Hundreds of thousands of Jews living in the Soviet Union desperately desired to leave their homes and move to other countries, especially Israel. The Soviet Union's policy of Jewish emigration followed a serpentine pattern of twists and turns. In 1979 they permitted 51,320 Soviet Jews to leave, but the number approved had dwindled to just 914 by 1986. The thousands of Jews waiting in line to leave needed a miracle.

Mikhail Gorbachev provided that miracle. His policy of *glasnost* (openness) improved the prospects of emigration for Soviet Jews. By 1987 exit visas were given to 8,011 Jews, and the trickle soon became a flood. The number swelled to more than 71,000 in 1989. By 1990 deteriorating economic conditions in the Soviet Union coupled with a rise in anti-Semitic violence caused the number of emigrants to rise to 200,000. Most of these individuals traveled to Israel.

Operation Moses and Operation Solomon

The mass exodus of Jews from the former Soviet Union to Israel over the last two decades has been nothing short of dramatic. But Jews from Russia are not the only ones returning to the land of Israel. The airlift of thousands of Ethiopian Jews to Israel in 1984 and 1991 reads like a plot from an action movie.

Tracing their ancestry to Jews who returned to Ethiopia with the Queen of Sheba, a pocket of nearly 30,000 Ethiopian Jews struggled amidst persecution in the land of Ethiopia. In 1973 the government of Israel traced the group's ancestry back to biblical times and confirmed their legal status as Jews.[2] A secret operation to airlift the Jews to Israel, named Operation Moses, began in 1984. The program spirited almost 12,000 Jews back to the land of Israel before word leaked out to the world. Under pressure from her Muslim neighbors, Ethiopia then halted the program.

Israel resumed the program in 1989, quietly flying several hundred Ethiopian Jews to the land of Israel each month. However, events in Ethiopia forced a change in plans. In the spring of 1991, Ethiopia's civil war lurched toward a climactic end. The Eritrean People's Liberation Front captured the capital of the

province of Eritrea, climaxing a thirty-year-old war
for Eritrean independence. At the same time, the army
of the Ethiopian People's Revolutionary Democratic
Front closed in on Addis Ababa, Ethiopia's capital.
The war trapped more than 16,000 Ethiopian Jews
who were still in the city waiting to be taken to Israel.

On Friday, May 24, 1991, Israel initiated Operation
Solomon. Over the next two days a plane loaded with
Ethiopian Jews took off every thirty minutes. When
the last plane took off from the tarmac in Addis
Ababa, a 2,900-year-old Jewish presence in Ethiopia
ended. Another group of Israel's descendants had
come home:

> Isaiah's prophecy has finally been fulfilled. All
> Israelites can now return to Canaan, the land of
> our forefathers.—Demelash Aysheshin[3]

Israel's Rebirth: Prophecy or Prelude?

Ezekiel had predicted that Israel would physically
return to the land promised by God to Abraham. He
also had predicted that they would return spiritually to
the God of Abraham. Many Jews today are returning
physically to the land of Israel, but they are not returning to the God of Israel. The return of Jews to Israel
today is not the fulfillment of Ezekiel's prophecy. But
if the present return is not the fulfillment of Ezekiel
36–37, does it have any prophetic significance?

I believe the answer is yes. While Ezekiel's prediction will not be fulfilled until Jesus returns to earth,
other prophets picture a time before the Messiah's
return when at least some Jews will be living in the

land. Two specific passages shed light on this partial return of Israel before Jesus' second coming.

What Time Is It?

Many sincere people panic when they begin reading the book of Daniel. Daniel's visions of statues and beasts seem so bizarre to us today. The images he presents remind us of characters from an old horror movie. As a result, many individuals become lost in the details and forget that God gave Daniel both his dreams and the interpretation.

Daniel 9 is God's timetable for the nation of Israel, and the background for the chapter comes from the Law of Moses. The people disobeyed God and reaped the harvest of their sin. One specific command Israel constantly violated was God's requirement for a "sabbatical year"—a time when the land was to lie fallow every seventh year (Leviticus 25:1-5). God threatened to cast Israel into a foreign country, where they would remain until the land enjoyed every sabbatical year omitted by the nation (26:33-35). In Deuteronomy 30, God announced that only when the people turned to Him in captivity and confessed their sins would He allow them to return to the land.

As Daniel studied the book of Jeremiah, he read the words of Jeremiah 25:11-12 and 29:10 that Judah's captivity in Babylon would last for seventy years. Nebuchadnezzar had seized Daniel and carried him to Babylon in 605 B.C. Daniel was reading this section of Jeremiah "in the first year of Darius son of Xerxes"— which was 538 B.C. Depending on the specific calendar being used by Daniel, this was the sixty-eighth or sixty-ninth year of his captivity! The time for Jeremiah's prophecy was very close! If the people would turn to God and repent of their sins, perhaps God would bring the final restoration promised to Moses in Deuteronomy 30.

Daniel dropped to his knees to pray for his rebellious brothers. "So I turned to the LORD God and pleaded with him in prayer and petition, in fasting, and in sackcloth and ashes" (Daniel 9:3). Anyone who wanted publicly to display sorrow or mourning would put on sackcloth—a coarse cloth that would cause discomfort—and would throw ashes on his head. The patriarch Jacob put on sackcloth when he thought wild beasts had slain his son Joseph (Genesis 37:31-35). When God confronted Job and challenged Job for his rash statements, Job responded by saying, "My ears had heard of you but now my eyes have seen you. Therefore I despise myself and repent in dust and ashes" (Job 42:5-6).

Daniel decided to intercede to God for all his fellow Israelites. He acknowledged God's righteousness and Israel's sin. When he referred specifically to "the curses and sworn judgments written in the Law of Moses" (Daniel 9:11), Daniel displayed his understanding of why his people were in exile. God had threatened to remove them from the land, and God had faithfully done just what He had said.

But beginning in verse 15, Daniel turns from the past to the present. In verses 15-19 Daniel prays for two specific items. First, he prays for "Jerusalem, your city, your holy hill" (v. 16). Jerusalem, Israel's capital city, lay in ruins. The "holy hill" was the hill in Jerusalem on which Solomon's temple had once sat. In verses 17-18, Daniel becomes even more specific as he asks God to "look with favor on your desolate sanctuary. . . . Open your eyes and see the desolation of the city that bears your Name." Daniel wanted God to restore the city of Jerusalem and to rebuild the temple.

But Daniel longed for more than just brick and mortar. His prayer focused on both places and people. Daniel asked God to help "Jerusalem and your people" (9:16). Concluding his plea, Daniel again linked Jerusalem and the Jews. "O LORD, listen! O LORD, forgive! O LORD, hear and act! For your sake, O my God, do not delay, because your city and your people bear your Name" (9:19).

God sent an angelic messenger to give God's answer to Daniel. "As soon as you began to pray, an answer was given, which I have come to tell you" (9:23). The vision that follows answers Daniel's prayer for Jerusalem and the Jews. However, God's answer at first seems very enigmatic: "Seventy 'sevens' are decreed for your people and your holy city" (9:24). God's answer solves the mystery of when Jerusalem and the Jews will finally be restored. But what are the "seventy sevens"?

When God said, "Seventy 'sevens' are decreed for your people and your holy city," what would Daniel have understood this to mean? Daniel provides the historical background for understanding the "seventy sevens" in the first two verses of the chapter. We know that Daniel was studying the book of Jeremiah and his prediction of the seventy-year captivity in Babylon. But why a seventy-year captivity? "The land enjoyed its sabbath rests; all the time of its desolation it rested, until the seventy years were completed in fulfillment of the word of the LORD spoken by Jeremiah" (2 Chronicles 36:21). Each year of captivity in Babylon represented a sabbatical year not observed when Israel had been in the land. As stated earlier, a sabbatical year came every seventh year, and during that year Israel was to let the land lie fallow. The Babylonian Captivity represented seventy sabbatical years. Evidently Israel had violated God's command at least seventy times in her history—a period that would have represented 490 years of disobedience.

When God announced that "seventy sevens" more would be required to complete Israel's restoration, what unit of measurement would have been in Daniel's mind? The logical answer is that Daniel would have thought of seventy sevens of sabbatical years. In effect God is telling Daniel that "seventy sevens" of years remain to be fulfilled before God fully restores Israel as a nation. God is providing Daniel with a timetable for the restoration of the Jews and Jerusalem.

God's prophetic clock does not begin ticking until "the issuing of the decree to restore and rebuild Jerusalem" (Daniel 9:25). Again, Daniel's focus is on the city. When was a command issued to restore and rebuild Jerusalem? Not until almost a century after Daniel penned God's promise. In 445 B.C., in the Hebrew month of Nisan (March/April), King Artaxerxes issued a decree in response to a request from his cupbearer, a Jew named Nehemiah. Though Jews had begun returning to the land of Israel ninety years earlier, Nehemiah was saddened by news of Jerusalem's continued desolation. He confided in the king, "Why should my face not look sad when the city where my fathers are buried lies in ruins, and its gates have been destroyed by fire?" (Nehemiah 2:3). Nehemiah finally asked the king, "If it pleases the king and if your servant has found favor in his sight, let him send me to the city in Judah where my fathers are buried so that I can rebuild it" (2:5).

"Know and understand this: From the issuing of the decree to restore and rebuild Jerusalem until the Anointed One, the ruler, comes, there will be seven 'sevens,' and sixty-two 'sevens'" (Daniel 9:25). The decree was issued in March/April 445 B.C. From the issuing of the decree until the Messiah (the "Anointed One") would be seven plus sixty-two groups of seven years. Seven plus sixty-two equals sixty-nine. Why did Daniel divide sixty-nine into two parts? Possibly he did it because the first part (seven "sevens") pointed to the time it would take to completely restore and rebuild Jerusalem. In any case, Daniel indicated that sixty-nine groups of seven years would click off between the issuing of the command and the arrival of the Messiah. Sixty-nine times seven equals 483 years.

Does this prediction by Daniel fit what we know about history? Yes it does, once we understand another clue from history—how the Jews measured time. Stop for a moment and think about our current calendar. Why does January have thirty-one days, while February has only twenty-eight? Why do we begin the new year on January 1? If we wanted to begin the new year on the shortest day of the year, we would move the date a week or so earlier to the first day of winter. Every fourth year we would add an extra day to the month of February to make our calendar come out even with the actual amount of time it takes the earth to revolve around the sun. And yet that still is not completely accurate. We do not add a leap year to the years that mark the even hundreds (1800, 1900, etc.) unless that year can be divided evenly by 400. Thus the year 1900 did not have a leap year, but the year 2000 will. Our calendar is complex, with many variables added to make it conform to the reality of the earth's movement around the sun. Yet we do not perceive it to be complex because we follow the normal pattern and take the exceptions (leap years, etc.) in stride with barely a second thought.

But how did the Jews count time? Generally, they followed the cycles of the moon and had twelve months each year that alternated between twenty-nine and thirty days in each month. Seven times during each nineteen-year period they would insert an extra month into the calendar to bring it back into conformity with the seasons. Just like us, they had a regular calendar and made the necessary adjustments in the calendar to bring it back into conformity with the actual movement of the earth around the sun.

Understanding how the Jews understood time is important to interpreting Daniel 9. When God announced that seventy sevens would be coming, how would the Jews have understood this in terms of actual months and days? Does the Bible provide us with any clues?

Amazingly enough, two other portions of the Bible help explain one part of Daniel 9. We will examine these in more detail later, but the passages can be listed here for comparison.

> He will confirm a covenant with many for one "seven." In the middle of the "seven" he will put an end to sacrifice and offering. And on a wing of the temple he will set up an abomination that causes desolation, until the end that is decreed is poured out on him. (Daniel 9:27)

> He will speak against the Most High and oppress his saints and try to change the set times and the laws. The saints will be handed over to him for a time, times and half a time. (Daniel 7:25)

> The woman fled into the desert to a place prepared for her by God, where she might be taken care of for 1,260 days. (Revelation 12:6)

> The beast was given a mouth to utter proud words and blasphemies and to exercise his authority for forty-two months. (Revelation 13:5)

Each of these passages describes the same period in the future when a satanically inspired world leader will try to destroy the Jews in a campaign of hatred against God. The time will continue for one-half of the final "seven" in Daniel 9. That would be for three-and-a-half years. This is the same amount of time called "a time, times and half a time" in Daniel 7. But more specifically, how much time is this in months and days? Revelation 13 describes the same time as a period of forty-two months. That would be accurate if, in looking ahead, the writer ignores the intercalary months that were inserted about every three years. Instead, the writer saw the time as three-and-a-half years of "normal" twelve-month years. Revelation 12 describes the same period as 1,260 days. That would only be true if the writer saw the time as ideal months with thirty days in each month. Forty-two months of thirty days each would equal 1,260 days.

When Daniel described God's future timetable for Israel, he used the calendar much like we do. If a bill is due in sixty days, we say that we have two months to pay. When talking about the future, we tend to group months into thirty-day segments. God described Israel's future to Daniel in the same way. From the time King Artaxerxes issued the command to restore and rebuild Jerusalem until the arrival of the Messiah would be 483 future years, which assumed twelve months each year with thirty days in each month. The time between the command and the Messiah would be 173,880 days.

According to some scholars, Jesus rode into Jerusalem exactly 173,880 days after Artaxerxes issued his decree to Nehemiah.[4] Jesus entered Jerusalem on a colt the way Zechariah said the Messiah would come (Zechariah 9:9), and He rode in on the day Daniel said the Messiah would come. Two of the Old Testament's most remarkable predictions were fulfilled on that day.

Daniel then describes a gap in God's timetable for Israel. Three specific events must happen during this break. First, "the Anointed One will be cut off and will have nothing" (Daniel 9:26). The Messiah—

Israel's promised King—would be killed and would not be allowed to assume His rightful place as king. Within days of crying "Hosanna to the Son of David" as He rode into Jerusalem, the fickle mob changed their cry to "Crucify him!" (Matthew 27:22).

God informs Daniel that a second event will take place during this break in His timetable. "The people of the ruler who will come will destroy the city and the sanctuary. The end will come like a flood" (Daniel 9:26). The "ruler who will come" refers to the final evil ruler described in more detail in the next verse. The nation from which this evil ruler ultimately emerges will destroy Jerusalem and the temple. Less than forty years after the mob gloated over the death of their Messiah, this awful event took place. In A.D. 70 the Romans broke through the defenses of Jerusalem and sacked the city. The city and temple whose rebuilding began this prophecy are once again decimated.

Daniel includes a third event in this gap: "War will continue until the end, and desolations have been decreed." During the remainder of this time the Jews will experience persecution, trouble, and hardship. This is a sad but accurate picture of the sufferings and persecutions that have haunted the Jews for the past two millennia.

Beginning in Daniel 9:27 the prophet picks up his stopwatch and again pushes the button to start the second hand moving. The final seven-year period begins with another specific action: "He will confirm a covenant with many for one 'seven'" (9:27). The *he* refers back to the "ruler who will come" in verse 26. The

Romans destroyed Jerusalem, and they were the nation from whom the "ruler who will come" would arise. Someone from the area that was once the Roman Empire will rise to rule the world. He will make some kind of agreement with Israel that is scheduled to last for seven years. The day he signs the agreement is the day that the final seven-year period begins.

The specifics of the agreement to be made with Israel will be examined in a later chapter. But the point to note here is that Israel must be back in the land as a nation before this agreement can be signed. This ruler cannot make a covenant or agreement with the nation if the nation is not in existence. Israel, at least partially, must be back in the land before the final seven-year period begins.

Jesus' Final Sermon

Nearly six centuries after Daniel made his predictions, Jesus rode into Jerusalem on the day Daniel had predicted. In the days that followed, Jesus confronted the religious rulers with their sin and hypocrisy and confounded His disciples by telling them of His imminent death. The disciples never fully grasped Jesus' explanation that He came first to be the Savior of the world, not just the Sovereign of the world. They were so excited at the time, looking forward to the kingdom, that they never grasped the necessity of the Cross.

During that final week before His crucifixion, Jesus led His band of followers on a daily hike between Jerusalem and the village of Bethany, where He spent the evenings. Hiking up the Mount of Olives, the disciples looked back at the magnificent temple constructed by Herod the Great. Jesus' words shocked His followers: "I tell you the truth, not one stone here will be left on another; every one will be thrown down" (Matthew 24:2). But how could this be? Wasn't Jesus' triumphal entry into Jerusalem the signal that the present age of Gentile domination was about to end and the Messiah's kingdom age about to begin?

The disciples paused to ask for clarification. They needed answers to two specific questions. First, "When will this happen?" (24:3). The disciples wanted to know the timing for Jerusalem's destruction and future glorification. They wanted to know when these events would take place. Second, they asked, "What will be the sign of your coming and of the end of the age?" (24:3). The disciples demanded to know the specific events they could watch for that would signal that His coming to set up the kingdom was near.

I believe Jesus answers both questions in this chapter, and He does so, in typical Jewish fashion, in reverse order. That is, the disciples asked Question A and then Question B. Jesus answered Question B first and then answered Question A. Jesus addressed the second question ("What will be the sign of your coming?") in 24:4-31, which ends with "the sign of the Son of Man" appearing in the sky. Beginning in 24:32 and going through 24:51, Jesus answered the first question ("When will this happen?"). He began by giving a general answer: "When you see all these things, you know that it is near" (24:33). Observing the events of the world will give His followers an approximate idea of the time of His return. However, He goes on to explain that they will not know the specific time. "Therefore keep watch, because you do not know the day or the hour" (25:13; also see verses 36, 42, and 44).

As Jesus explained to His disciples the signs and events that will foreshadow His return to establish His kingdom, He described a time of trouble that will precede His return. This period will begin with the construction of a statue in the temple. "So when you see standing in the holy place 'the abomination that causes desolation,' spoken of through the prophet Daniel—let the reader understand—then let those who are in Judea flee to the mountains" (24:15-16). Jesus is pointing His disciples back to the prophecy of Daniel 9! Daniel wrote that the coming ruler would make a seven-year agreement. But in the middle of that time he would break the agreement and "put an end to sacrifice and offering. And on a wing of the temple he will set up an abomination that causes desolation" (Daniel 9:27).

As Jesus described the events still awaiting fulfillment, He reminded the disciples of Daniel's prophecy. That prophecy was still future. Jesus assumed two points. First, He assumed that the temple (which He already said would be destroyed) would be rebuilt. It must be rebuilt so the "abomination that causes desolation" can be erected "in the holy place." Second, He assumed that the Jews would be in the land of Israel when this event takes place. They must be there because Jesus warns "those who are in Judea" to flee for safety when the statue is set up.

First Steps

Israel will someday experience the blessings promised to her by God. All Jews will return to the land and call it home. Their physical restoration will be matched by a spiritual renewal. In returning to the land, they will acknowledge Jesus as their Messiah and will receive forgiveness of their sins and the indwelling presence of God's Holy Spirit. This will be the day when Ezekiel's valley of dry bones will finally come to life. It also will be the day when Daniel's timetable for Israel will be completed.

Israel today is not fulfilling these promises. However, they are in the land as part of God's larger plans for the end times. Before God's final seven-year schedule begins, Israel must, at least partially, be back in the land. Then the nation must make a covenant with the future prince of trouble, who will turn on the nation midway through this seven-year agreement.

Israel's return to the land in 1948 sets the stage for God's final prophetic drama. A partial exodus has begun, and everything is in place for the end times to begin. However, the final exodus will not take place until Jesus Christ, the Messiah, returns to earth to set up His kingdom. Only then will the final peace and security that Israel so desperately seeks be possible. But the elusive nature of a lasting peace has not kept many from trying to achieve it.

CHAPTER FOUR
WHAT PRICE PEACE?

The date for Israel's rebirth as a nation was Friday, May 14, 1948. But the nation's birth was not without complications. Surrounding Israel were seven nations who publicly opposed the creation of the Jewish state. From the day she was born, Israel has remained in a state of war with most of her Arab neighbors, who (except for Egypt) refuse to acknowledge her existence.

Only days before Israel became a nation, her leaders tried in vain to forge a peaceful settlement with her enemies. Golda Meir, later one of Israel's most dynamic prime ministers, made a secret journey to Amman, Jordan. Dressed as an Arab with her face veiled, Golda Meir visited King Abdullah of Jordan to find a peaceful way for Israel and Jordan to live together. Both wanted to make peace, but King Abdullah was trapped, a victim of war fervor that had gripped the Arab masses. As Mrs. Meir left, she recalled the king's last, sad words. "I am sorry. I deplore the coming bloodshed and destruction. Let us hope we shall meet again and not sever relations."[1] They never saw one another again.

If at First You Don't Succeed

Golda Meir may have been the first to attempt to make peace between Israel and the Arabs, but she was not the last. World leaders advanced a myriad of plans and proposals for bringing peace to the Middle East, but none have been completely successful. Henry Kissinger began his shuttle diplomacy following the 1973 Yom Kippur War. He forged a cease-fire between Israel and Egypt, but he could not bring lasting peace to the Middle East.

Egyptian president Anwar Sadat's historic trip to Jerusalem in November 1977 for face-to-face talks with Israel's prime minister Menachem Begin raised great hopes for a final, lasting peace in the Middle East. The following year the two men met with President Jimmy Carter at Camp David in Maryland for thirteen days of intense negotiations that produced the Camp David Peace Accord on September 17, 1978. On April 25, 1979, they formally ratified the treaty, and Egypt became the first Arab country to recognize Israel's right to exist as a nation. But other Arab nations refused to follow Egypt's lead. Instead, they ostracized Egypt, and Anwar Sadat was assassinated.

The 1991 Gulf War revived the peace process. Following the defeat of Iraq, U.S. Secretary of State James Baker made four separate journeys to the Middle East in just two months. His marathon search for peace produced the first face-to-face meetings between Israel and her Arab neighbors since Israel became a nation. Will the U.S. government finally succeed where all others have failed, or have these negotiations been just another attempt to resolve an unresolvable dispute?

The Coming False Peace

The Bible predicts that a temporary time of peace will sweep the world, especially the Middle East, as a prelude to God's end-time events. The Apostle Paul wrote two letters to a new church in the city of Thessalonica. In both letters he provided insight into what the future would hold for these believers and for the rest of the world. In 1 Thessalonians 5 Paul explains how God's end-time judgment will come on the world: "For you know very well that the day of the Lord will come like a thief in the night. While people are saying, 'Peace and safety,' destruction will come on them suddenly, as labor pains on a pregnant woman, and they will not escape" (1 Thessalonians 5:2-3).

Paul explained to the Thessalonians that God's end-time judgment will catch the world unaware. God's torrent of trouble will descend like a raging flood on an unsuspecting world basking in a false sense of security and well-being. Proclamations of peace are the prelude to judgment.

In Israel today, peace is only the absence of war or terrorism. After four decades and five major wars, Israel still cannot lower her guard. Two scenes from life in the Middle East drove this point home to me most dramatically. The first scene took place in a merchant's shop in Amman, Jordan. While looking at mother-of-pearl boxes, I glanced at a map partially hidden on the far wall. Walking closer I saw that it was a map of the Middle East in Arabic and English. The map highlighted Israel in black, but the word *Israel* did not appear. Instead, the words *Occupied Arab Territory* blazed from the blackened silhouette.

The second scene took place in the Ben Gurion airport in Tel Aviv. An Arab passenger stood just in front of me waiting in line to go through the security check. The security officer opened the man's suitcase and dumped the contents on the table. He hand-checked every article of clothing and threw them onto a pile as he finished. But he was still not done. He carried away the empty suitcase to have the lining X-rayed. Only then could the unfortunate traveler gather up his belongings and try to repack his suitcase. Such is the hatred and distrust between Israel and the Arabs.

But the prophet Ezekiel describes a time when Israel will experience far different conditions. Ezekiel envisions a time when Israel will be called "a land that has recovered from war," and the people will be described as those who "had been brought out from the nations, and now all of them live in safety" (Ezekiel 38:8). Ezekiel paints a graphic picture of this time of peace a few verses later. There he describes the nation as "a land of unwalled villages" with "a peaceful and unsuspecting people—all of them living without walls and without gates and bars" (38:11). Ezekiel writes that this period of peace will be shattered when a group of nations launch a surprise attack against unsuspecting Israel.

The scene described by Ezekiel has never happened historically, but when will it be true of the nation of Israel? Ezekiel supplies some clues that help us nar-

row the time. First, while he does describe a time
when the nation is back in the land and dwelling in
safety, he pointedly notes that the events he describes
occur sometime before all Jews return to the land. One
result of the failed attack is the ultimate restoration of
all Jews to the land of Israel. After describing how
God will destroy the invaders, Ezekiel notes that God
will use His victory to restore all Jews to the land. "I
will now bring Jacob back from captivity and will
have compassion on all the people of Israel, and I will
be zealous for my holy name" (39:25).

Second, Ezekiel explains that one result of the invasion described in these chapters is that the nation of
Israel will come to know her God. "From that day forward the house of Israel will know that I am the LORD
their God" (39:22). As Israel turns to her God, He
responds by pouring His Holy Spirit on His people. "I
will no longer hide my face from them, for I will pour
out my Spirit on the house of Israel, declares the Sovereign LORD" (39:29). In Ezekiel 36–37 (discussed in
chapter 3) the prophet announced that God would
pour out His Holy Spirit on the people and restore all
the nation to the land when He inaugurates His earthly
kingdom. The events of Ezekiel 38–39 must precede
that event.

So when do the events of Ezekiel 38–39 take place?
They take place after Jews have returned to the land
and established the nation of Israel. They also take
place in a time when Israel finally feels at peace and
secure. However, the events occur before Israel experi-
ences her ultimate physical and spiritual restoration.
In fact, the events of these chapters are instrumental in

bringing all Jews to an intimate knowledge of their God so that He can fully restore the nation. The period that best fits these particular characteristics is the first half of the final seven-year period described in Daniel 9:27.

Ezekiel's portrait of Israel at peace seems so remote today. How will the nation ever reach a point where it feels this secure? Daniel 9:27 gives the likely answer: "He will confirm a covenant with many for one 'seven.' In the middle of the 'seven' he will put an end to sacrifice and offering." The final seven-year period of Israel's 480-year wait for her kingdom begins with a treaty. The antecedent of "he" in verse 27 is "the ruler who will come" in verse 26. The Romans destroyed Jerusalem in A.D. 70. These Roman invaders were "the people of the ruler who will come." Therefore, "the ruler who will come" must come from the territory of the original Roman Empire.

This ruler will make a "covenant" or agreement with Israel for seven years. Part of the agreement allows Israel to build her temple and resume animal sacrifices. The covenant also must provide protection and security for the nation of Israel. Under the terms of this agreement, Israel will finally appear to achieve lasting peace in secure borders. This coming ruler will succeed where Henry Kissinger, Jimmy Carter, and James Baker failed. He will likely be nominated for the Nobel Peace Prize. He will be the Antichrist!

Israel longs for peace and security—precious commodities in the Middle East. Until the beginning of the 1991 Gulf War, Israel had relied primarily on her ability and military might to maintain her independence. The Gulf War was remarkable in that for the first time Israel allowed others to fight her battles. Soldiers from the United States operated the Patriot missile batteries. The planes bombing Baghdad and hunting for mobile missile launchers came from the United States and her coalition Allies—not from Israel. Other nations fought to protect Israel from attack.

Will the peace talks sponsored by the United States government produce a lasting peace between Israel and her Arab neighbors? David Dolan, a Middle East correspondent for CBS Radio and a firsthand observer of the Arab/Israeli conflict, is not optimistic. "Yet friend and foe alike should also be prepared to concede that there may not be a man-made solution to the intense Arab/Israeli conflict. This is basically the conclusion I have come to after a decade of studying the conflict, not in some classroom, but in the places where it is played out every day."[2]

Israel and her Arab neighbors may not willingly come to an agreement because neither side trusts the other. Could it be possible that any "final solution" to the current Middle East crisis will need to be brokered by an outside power who will be willing to "guarantee" Israel's security while Israel and her Arab neighbors implement the treaty? Daniel 9:27 does not say specifically what type of "covenant" will be made with Israel. But the passage very clearly states that the parties making the agreement expect it to last seven years. It is during the first part of this seven-year period when Israel feels, for the first time since returning to the land, a sense of safety and security. Could the agreement be a peace treaty designed to normalize relations between Israel and her Arab neighbors over a seven-year period with some type of international peace-keeping force guaranteeing secure borders? This is one likely scenario.

When Will Peace Come?

The world longs for peace. But when will the peace promised by God actually come? Many passages in the Bible provide God's answer, but the first twelve chapters of Isaiah provide one of the most compelling. In the first five chapters Isaiah acts as God's prosecuting attorney as he calls Judah to the witness stand. God lodges three specific charges against the nation in chapter 1. Their underlying sin is rebellion against God: "I reared children and brought them up, but they have rebelled against me" (Isaiah 1:2). The people reveal their rebellion in the way they hypocritically pretend to worship God while refusing to follow His teachings. "When you spread out your hands in prayer, I will hide my eyes from you; even if you offer many prayers, I will not listen. Your hands are full of blood" (1:15). Their rebellion also surfaces in the way they mistreat their fellow citizens and pervert justice. "Your rulers are rebels, companions of thieves; they all love bribes and chase after gifts. They do not defend the cause of the fatherless; the widow's case does not come before them" (1:23).

God pronounced the nation guilty on all counts. But God's desire was to heal, not to punish. In a tender attempt to woo the nation back, God pleads with the

nation, "'Come now, let us reason together,' says the
LORD. 'Though your sins are like scarlet, they shall be
as white as snow; though they are red as crimson, they
shall be like wool'" (1:18). In chapter 2 Isaiah
describes the time when God will bring Israel to this
place of forgiveness and blessing. Isaiah calls the time
"the last days" and says that in those days God will
reestablish His worldwide blessing. "He will judge between the nations and will settle disputes for many
peoples. They will beat their swords into plowshares
and their spears into pruning hooks. Nation will not
take up sword against nation, nor will they train for
war anymore" (2:4).

The United Nations has inscribed Isaiah's words on
their building in New York, but the world still has an
abundance of swords and a shortage of plowshares!
When will God bring His universal peace to a war-
weary world? Isaiah writes that peace will come with
the birth of a child. In Isaiah 7–12 the prophet predicts
the coming of a child who will bring peace. The
child's name is Immanuel—"God with us" (7:14)—
but He also will be called "Wonderful Counselor,
Mighty God, Everlasting Father, Prince of Peace"
(9:6). This child is both God and King: "He will reign
on David's throne and over his kingdom, establishing
and upholding it with justice and righteousness from
that time on and forever" (9:7).

This God/man will reign as king on David's throne
and will bring peace to the world. Isaiah pictures a
peace so pervasive that even the animal kingdom will
live together in harmony: "The wolf will live with the
lamb, the leopard will lie down with the goat, the calf

and the lion and the yearling together; and a little child will lead them. . . . They will neither harm nor destroy on all my holy mountain, for the earth will be full of the knowledge of the LORD as the waters cover the sea" (11:6-9).

True world peace will only come when the Prince of Peace returns to establish His kingdom. All other efforts, no matter how sincere, will not produce a lasting peace.

CHAPTER FIVE
THE THIRD TEMPLE

Jerusalem. October 8, 1990. Iraq's invasion of Kuwait
was only sixty-eight days old. The Bush administration was carefully constructing a coalition of nations
to put international pressure on Saddam Hussein.
Because the United States had always been Israel's
main ally, delicate negotiations were necessary to
forge an alliance that included the other Arab nations.
But events that swirled out of control on an elevated
platform on the southeast corner of the Old City of
Jerusalem almost shattered the alliance.

The city of Jerusalem epitomizes the problems that
plague the Middle East. It is a city of conflict and con-
tradiction. King David's original city of Jerusalem
now lies outside the walls of the current "Old City."
The El-Aksa mosque and the Dome of the Rock—
buildings sacred to the Islamic faith—stand on an arti-
ficial platform constructed two millennia ago by
Herod the Great to serve as the site for the temple of
Israel. "Mount Zion," the name that described both
the original city of Jerusalem and the temple precincts,
now describes a hill that has nothing to do with either

location. The name "migrated" to a mountain that only became part of Jerusalem proper during the reign of King Hezekiah, 250 years after the time of David.

On October 8, 1990, the government leaders in Washington, D.C., held their collective breath. The eyes of the world momentarily shifted from Kuwait to Jerusalem, and for a brief instant many questioned the ability of the United States to fashion a unified coalition. What momentous event almost caused the collapse of the Allied coalition? A riot that resulted from the actions of a handful of Jews carrying a block of limestone!

The Massacre on the Mount

A small group of Jews, called the Temple Mount Faithful, marched toward the temple mount platform on which the Dome of the Rock and the El-Aksa mosque now rest. Their desire was to put in place the foundation stone for the rebuilding of Judaism's Third Temple. Solomon constructed the First Temple on Mount Moriah, the hill just north of David's Jerusalem where Abraham originally journeyed to offer up his son Isaac. The Babylonians destroyed Solomon's temple when they burned Jerusalem in 586 B.C. The Jewish remnant that returned to Jerusalem seventy years later constructed the Second Temple. Herod the Great made extensive revisions to this temple, and it was an object of beauty and appreciation in Jesus' day. The Romans demolished the Second Temple when they destroyed Jerusalem in A.D. 70. Only the platform on which the temple rested still remains.

Religious Jews still look for a Third Temple—a

temple to be built when the Messiah comes and restores Israel to her land. Some feel that the temple will not be rebuilt until the Messiah returns, but others believe that the Messiah will not return until the Jews complete their temple. Thus the Temple Mount Faithful, along with other Jewish groups, want to begin the process of rebuilding the temple as soon as possible.

On October 8, 1990, the United States was observing Columbus Day. Banks and federal offices were closed, though the Gulf crisis forced many government officials to remain on the job. But in Israel the date held more significance. The evening of September 20 had signaled the start of the Jewish New Year—Rosh Hashanah—beginning year 5750 on the Hebrew calendar. Nine days later, on the evening of September 29, the Jews celebrated their holiest day of the year, Yom Kippur, the Day of Atonement. Five days later, on the evening of October 4, they began to celebrate the third fall festival held in the Jewish month Tishri—the Feast of Tabernacles (also called the Feast of Booths or Feast of Ingathering). This seven-day festival celebrates the end of the harvest season. But it also looks back to the time when Israel dwelt in the wilderness with Moses, a period when they were not in possession of their Promised Land. The festival also points forward to the time when Israel will possess their land fully. The Temple Mount Faithful chose to lay the foundation for the Third Temple in the middle of the Feast of Tabernacles—the very feast that looks forward to the final ingathering of the nation to their land.

The Israeli civil authorities, sensitive to the consequences of such an action on events in the Middle East, denied the group permission to carry the foundation stone to the temple mount. But word spread among the Arab population that the Jews were coming to lay their foundation stone and desecrate Islam's holy shrines. Crowds of angry Arabs gathered on the site to protect their holy shrines from the perceived threat. They collected rocks and stones to hurl at anyone who would dare defile their sacred sites. As the Arabs gathered above, thousands of unsuspecting Jews were crowding into the plaza before the Western Wall—the southwestern portion of the retaining wall built by Herod the Great. For centuries this spot was the closest any Jews could come to the site of the temple, and it remains a most sacred spot for Judaism.

The massing of Jews in the plaza below and Arabs on the platform above provided a volatile combination. Accounts differ, but something or someone incited the Arabs to hurl rocks down from the platform into the plaza below. Jewish riot police stormed the temple mount area, and when the riot was over seventeen Arabs had died. The death toll eventually rose to twenty-one.

The United Nations Security Council debated the event and passed a resolution condemning Israel. To hold together the coalition against Saddam Hussein, the United States went along with the resolution. The incident did not destroy the coalition, but it did focus world attention on Israel, on the religious nature of the conflict between Arabs and Jews, and on the centrality of the temple mount in the division.

Do the Jews Want a Temple?

Why build a temple? Since Israel's captivity in Babylon, the synagogue has become the focus for Jewish religious life. With the destruction of the Second Temple in A.D. 70, the synagogue has been the sole place of worship for Jews scattered around the world. More than 1,900 years have passed since Israel last had a temple. Yet the longing for the central sanctuary has not waned.

Until 1967 any desire to rebuild the temple was only a faint glimmer in the darkness of reality. For the past thirteen centuries the Islamic faith dominated the city and the temple mount. Except for a brief period during the Crusades, the Muslims have maintained control over the site. They refused to allow Jews to pray on the temple mount. The closest the Jews could come was the small section of wall on the southwest corner. The Western Wall or Wailing Wall was an imperfect substitute for the lost temple.

But everything changed in 1967. With the capture of the Old City of Jerusalem in the Six-Day War, Israel finally had control over their ancient capital. Yet, to avoid a holy war, the government has refused to modify any of the holy sites. Muslims still administer the temple mount, but a growing number of Jews want to rebuild the temple in Israel. In a 1983 newspaper poll, 18.3 percent of Israelis felt that the time was right to rebuild the temple.[1]

In 1989, Israel's Ministry of Religious Affairs was host to a Conference of Temple Research. Groups have formed to prepare the articles of clothing and the utensils that would be needed in a rebuilt temple.

These items are on display in a museum at the Temple Institute in Jerusalem. In a booklet explaining their purpose, the Temple Institute shows its longing for a rebuilt temple:

> The dream of rebuilding the Temple spans 50 generations of Jews, five continents and innumerable seas and oceans. . . . With G-d's help we will soon be able to rebuild the Temple on its holy mountain in Jerusalem, ushering in an era of peace and understanding, love and kindness, when "G-d will be king over all the earth, in that day G-d will be one and his name will be one."[2]

Work goes on to breed the red heifer and to prepare the necessary articles and clothing to rebuild the temple. Some erroneous reports have said that Israel is secretly stockpiling marble and limestone blocks for the building, but those reports appear to be groundless. Still, some groups, though they represent a small minority, are making serious preparations to rebuild the temple and resume its worship. But how can a temple be built on land already occupied by Muslim mosques and shrines?

We'll Make It Fit

Religious Jews today are forbidden to set foot on the temple mount because the exact location of the temple proper is still not known. The rabbis fear that a Jew could unknowingly step in the Holy Place or the Holy of Holies, where the ark of the covenant once rested. Before the temple can be rebuilt, its exact location on the temple mount will need to be determined. However, the Arabs will not permit any archaeological excavations on the temple mount—especially not if those excavations lead to a Jewish temple!

A lack of access to the temple mount has not hindered some from using other means to try to locate the temple itself. Excavations have been done along the side of the temple mount. This tunnel, called the Rabbinical Tunnel, extends 900 feet along the Western Wall under the city. Others have examined ancient sources, including Josephus and the Dead Sea Scrolls, for clues about the location of the temple. They hope to find enough historical data to position the temple itself on the temple mount.

Asher Kaufman, an orthodox Jewish immigrant from Scotland, made a complete study of the available historical data. In a remarkable article in *Biblical Archaeology Review,* Kaufman argues that the ancient Holy of Holies was not located over the Dome of the Rock. Instead, he suggests that the Holy of Holies stood approximately a hundred yards farther north on the temple mount.[3] Kaufman uses mostly literary sources to make his conclusions, but he does offer some preliminary archaeological support for his view.

No major archaeologist in Israel finds Asher Kaufman's views convincing, but the point here is not to argue whether Kaufman's views are correct. Many Orthodox Jews are poring over every scrap of data, trying to find where the temple stood. If they conclude that Kaufman's position fits the evidence, then they will build the temple where he has suggested. But if the religious community rejects his views, they will build their temple based on their interpretation of ancient written sources and traditions more than on the assertions of archaeologists. Certainly this would not be the first time that tradition and archaeology have clashed. Jews today have a synagogue at the traditional tomb of David, though all archaeologists would agree that the tomb is not authentic. (It's not even on the right mountain in Jerusalem!)

Other scholars believe the original temple was located on the site now occupied by the Dome of the Rock. Leen Ritmeyer, an architect, archaeologist, and historian, pieced together clues from archaeology and history to offer the latest theory on the location of the temple. He argues convincingly that the specific spot where the ark rested in the Holy of Holies was on a platform built over Es-Sakhra, the rock formation on which the Dome of the Rock is built.[4] If Ritmeyer's conclusions are accepted, the Dome of the Rock will need to be demolished before the temple can be rebuilt.

Will the Arabs Permit a Temple?

Today prospects seem remote for a rebuilt temple on its original site. The mere rumor of a group of Jews coming to lay a foundation stone is enough to bring out thousands of angry demonstrators. Arabs have vowed to fight to the last drop of Arab blood to protect the third holiest site in all Islam. And yet small groups of Jews are equally insistent that they will build the Third Temple on its original spot. How can this be resolved?

God does not provide specific details on how such

a situation can be resolved, but He is clear in saying that a new temple will be built. The temple does not have to be built before the clock begins ticking on God's final seven-year program for the nation of Israel. But it must be built within the first half of that seven-year period. God provides a three-and-a-half-year window during which the temple building will be constructed.

In Daniel 9 (a passage discussed in some detail in chapters 3 and 4) the prophet described Israel's final 490-year future, which extended from the time the command came to rebuild Jerusalem until the fulfillment of God's kingdom promises. The final seven-year period is still future and begins when the coming world ruler makes a covenant, or agreement, with Israel. But "in the middle of the 'seven' he will put an end to sacrifice and offering. And in a wing of the temple he will set up an abomination that causes desolation" (Daniel 9:27). For this passage to be fulfilled the temple will need to be rebuilt with the sacrificial system in operation.

More than five centuries after Daniel made his prediction, this prophecy had not yet been fulfilled. Jesus explained to His disciples that the event was still future. He also provided additional information: "So when you see standing in the holy place 'the abomination that causes desolation,' spoken of through the prophet Daniel—let the reader understand—then let those who are in Judea flee to the mountains" (Matthew 24:15-16). Jesus reminds His disciples that the event predicted by Daniel will begin the final time of trouble for the nation of Israel. Jesus specifically says that the sign will be revealed "in the holy place"—a clear reference to the temple that must exist then.

Nearly twenty years after Jesus explained the end times to His disciples, the Apostle Paul gave a similar explanation to a new group of believers in Greece. In his second letter to the Thessalonians, Paul explained to his readers that they were not yet living in the end times. Evidently someone had sent the church a letter stating that the final days predicted by Daniel and Jesus were already upon them. In 2 Thessalonians 2:2, Paul instructs his readers "not to become easily unsettled or alarmed by some prophecy, report or letter supposed to have come from us, saying that the day of the Lord has already come."

Paul then traces the events that God's Word had already revealed:

> Don't let anyone deceive you in any way, for that day will not come until the rebellion occurs and the man of lawlessness is revealed, the man doomed to destruction. He will oppose and will exalt himself over everything that is called God or is worshiped, so that he sets himself up in God's temple, proclaiming himself to be God. (2 Thessalonians 2:3-4)

Again the sequence is clear. The "man of sin" will be revealed at the start of the final prophetic period. He will go to the temple in Jerusalem and proclaim himself to be God. This act starts the final three-and-a-half years of trouble.

Daniel, Jesus, and Paul all pointed to the same historic event. But could that event have been fulfilled when the Romans destroyed Jerusalem in A.D. 70? The Apostle John answers with a resounding *no!* Forty years after Paul wrote to the Thessalonians (and twenty-five years after Jerusalem fell to the Romans), the Apostle John announced that the fulfillment of the prophecies of Daniel, Jesus, and Paul was still future.

In Revelation 12–13 John describes the trio of trouble who will plague the earth in the last days. The supreme leader of this trio is "that ancient serpent called the devil, or Satan, who leads the whole world astray" (Revelation 12:9). In chapter 12 John informs his readers that spiritual forces will be very visible during the final days. Satan will seek to persecute the nation of Israel. Israel, pictured as a woman, will be forced to flee "into the desert," possibly picturing the rugged, dry Judean wilderness or the wilderness of the Sinai peninsula. John writes that Israel will find divine protection in this time of persecution that will last "for 1,260 days" (Revelation 12:6). Using the Hebrew calendar, John is describing a time of persecution that will last for three-and-a-half years (1,260 days, or 42 months of 30 days each).

If the first member of the trio of trouble is Satan, who is the second? John writes that the second member of the trio will be the future world leader who will be empowered by Satan. John describes this leader as a "beast," drawing on the description given in Daniel 7. This leader will become the dominant military power in the end times. The whole world will ask, "Who is like the beast? Who can make war against him?" (Revelation 13:4). Again, John identifies this

beast with the end-time leader described by Daniel.
Daniel predicted that this ruler would make a seven-
year treaty, break it in the middle, and then persecute
Israel for the remaining time. John describes the same
events:

> The beast was given a mouth to utter proud
> words and blasphemies and to exercise his
> authority for forty-two months. He opened his
> mouth to blaspheme God, and to slander his
> name and his dwelling place and those who live
> in heaven. He was given power to make war
> against the saints and to conquer them. (Revela-
> tion 13:5-7)

Forty-two months, 1,260 days, three-and-a-half
years—Daniel and John are describing the same
events.

John then introduces the third member of the trio of
trouble. He describes him as "another beast. . . . He
had two horns like a lamb, but he spoke like a dragon"
(Revelation 13:11). The final member of this trio
seems to be a religious figure who is gentle and Christ-
like ("like a lamb") but who really finds his message
and his power from Satan ("like a dragon"). The role
of this individual is to encourage the world to worship
the future world leader—he "made the earth and its
inhabitants worship the first beast" (13:12). But how
will he do this?

John provides the key, and in doing so he explains
in more detail the message of Daniel, Jesus, and Paul.
This third member of the trio will deceive the earth.

"He ordered them to set up an image in honor of the beast who was wounded by the sword and yet lived. He was given power to give breath to the image of the first beast, so that it could speak and cause all who refused to worship the image to be killed" (13:14-15).

The "abomination that causes desolation" will be a statue of the future world leader. The statue will be set up in the temple in Jerusalem. Through a satanic counterfeit miracle, the statue will seem to come to life. A voice from the statue will demand that the world worship the world leader as God. Anyone refusing will be put to death. Is it any wonder that when Jesus told His disciples about this event, He warned them to "flee to the mountains" when the abomination is established? They were not even to take the time to pack or to dress.

These prophets unite in describing events that will occur in the temple in Jerusalem in the middle of the final seven-year period coming on the earth. Evidently the temple will be rebuilt during the first half of the seven-year period and will be in operation. The holy place will be built, and animal sacrifices will be resumed. Is three-and-a-half years enough time to build a temple?

Solomon's first temple took seven years to build (1 Kings 6:38). Following the destruction of Solomon's temple and the captivity in Babylon, the Jews started to rebuild the temple in 536 B.C. Work began on the foundation, but local opposition halted all activity shortly afterward. The temple remained in ruins until 520 B.C. when God raised up the prophets Haggai and Zechariah to spur the people on. The foundation was relaid beginning on September 21, 520 B.C. (Haggai 1:15), and the temple was completed on March 12, 516 B.C.—in three-and-a-half years! Given modern construction methods and the importance of the project, one could envision a temple built and in operation in three-and-a-half years.

A temple will be constructed sometime in the future. Since the temple mount is also home to two Muslim shrines, how will this be accomplished? God does not say, so any suggestions are merely speculation. Perhaps an earthquake will destroy the Dome of the Rock. Perhaps the Jews will risk Arab anger and tear the structure down. Perhaps the views of Asher Kaufman will be accepted and the temple will be rebuilt on the temple mount without disturbing the Muslim holy places.

The most likely suggestion is that the future world leader will allow the Jews to construct a sanctuary as part of his seven-year treaty with them. God's Word does not tell us how Israel will obtain permission to rebuild her temple, but it clearly predicts that Israel will rebuild the temple. The temple will become home to the "abomination that causes desolation." The "house of God" will become the headquarters for the trio of trouble.

CHAPTER SIX
THE FINAL HOLOCAUST

The sun dipped lower in the sky as our bus drove down the road leading to Yad Vashem—Israel's Holocaust memorial. The day had been hectic but rewarding. All morning we had walked through the Old City of Jerusalem. The hike ended at the Gihon Spring— the starting point for a remarkable walk through Hezekiah's Tunnel. The cold water was mid-thigh deep as we felt our way through the tunnel snaking under the ancient city of Jerusalem. Just after lunch we had driven to the model of the Second Temple in Jerusalem at the Holy Land Hotel. The clear sky and small crowds had given our group an excellent opportunity to snap pictures of the model. Now, as we approached our final stop of the day, the group was tired but happy. This had been a full and fun day.

As we stepped from the bus and walked up the pathway to the building, the dramatic relief on the side of the building caught my eye. At first I thought it was a representation of the captives being taken from Jerusalem following its fall to Titus in A.D. 70. But as I gazed at the line of silent sentinels silhouetted on the wall, I realized that they were meshed in barbed wire with Nazi guards. And they were marching not to captivity but to concentration camps.

Yad Vashem's simplicity impressed me. No fancy computer-generated graphics or glitzy animation. Instead we wound our way through pictures and posters providing firsthand accounts of Nazi persecution before and during World War II. The fact that the Nazis had seen fit to photograph and film the atrocities, as if they were documenting the eradication of some loathsome disease, magnified the horror.

I wandered through the exhibit trying to absorb the enormity of what I was seeing. I struggled to control my sadness and anger over the millions who lost their lives for the "sin" of being born Jewish. I managed to repress my emotions until I reached the end of the museum. Just before leaving I stopped to read a display that graphically portrayed the number of Jews killed in the various countries during the Nazi occupation. At the very end stood a glass display case holding a single child's shoe. Above the case was the statistic—1.5 million children killed. The shoe looked as though it would fit the foot of my oldest child. And as I thought about the son I loved so much, the revulsion of what had taken place overwhelmed me.

Our group boarded the bus in silence. I could not talk about what I had just seen—I was afraid that I might begin to cry. But as we drove away I felt as though I now had more insight into why the nation of Israel reacts the way it does to any and every external threat. Those who have suffered so much are determined to make sure it will never happen again.

The Satanic Source of Anti-Semitism

Why have the Jews suffered so much over the centuries? The danger is to offer simplistic answers to a complex issue. Certainly some of Israel's past suffering stems from her covenant relationship to God. At Mount Sinai Israel made an agreement with God. God set up specific requirements for His people. In Leviticus 26 God provided His people with a list of blessings for obedience and cursings, or punishments, for disobedience. He repeated His list of blessings and cursings to a new generation in Deuteronomy 28.

God's point in threatening Israel with these curses was to remind the nation of the consequences they would experience for breaking their covenant with Him. The final cursing threatened by God was expulsion from the land of Israel and persecution by other nations in foreign lands. "Then the LORD will scatter you among all nations, from one end of the earth to the other. . . . Among those nations you will find no repose, no resting place for the sole of your foot" (28:64-65). In short, some of Israel's suffering came as the direct result of her disobedience to God. But does this explain why the Jews have suffered for so long?

Some so-called Christians have persecuted the Jews in the name of Christ. Misinterpreting the cry of the mob described in Matthew 27:25, "Let his blood be on us and on our children," these misguided zealots have blamed the Jews for the death of Jesus. In the name of Christ these individuals have terrorized and brutalized the Jews. From the Russian pogroms to the Nazi Holocaust to some anti-Jewish harassment in

Germany and the United States today, much of the anti-Semitic hatred comes bearing the banner of the cross.

Many have persecuted the Jews in the name of Christ, but such actions deny the very Lord whom they claim. Today's Jews are not responsible for the death of Jesus. Before being seized and crucified, Jesus told His disciples that He had to die for the sins of the world: "This is my blood of the covenant, which is poured out for many for the forgiveness of sins" (26:28). When captured, Jesus reminded His attackers that He was willingly allowing Himself to be seized: "Do you think I cannot call on my Father, and he will at once put at my disposal more than twelve legions of angels?" (26:53). The Jews are not responsible for the death of Jesus; He willingly allowed Himself to be put to death.

Jesus died, not because the Jews killed Him, but because our sin demanded payment. The prophet Isaiah, gazing into the future, saw who was ultimately responsible for the death of Jesus—and he saw you and me.

> Surely he took up our infirmities and carried our sorrows, yet we considered him stricken by God, smitten by him, and afflicted. But he was pierced for our transgressions, he was crushed for our iniquities; the punishment that brought us peace was upon him, and by his wounds we are healed. We all, like sheep, have gone astray, each of us has turned to his own way; and the LORD has laid on him the iniquity of us all. (Isaiah 53:4-6)

God allowed His Son to die for your sins and mine. We are as responsible for nailing Jesus to the cross as any Jew that stood in the crowd before Pilate calling for Jesus' crucifixion.

If anti-Semitism cannot be attributed to God punishing the Jews for the death of Jesus, then what is the source of such hatred for the Jews? The Apostle John answers the enigma in Revelation 12 as he pulls back the curtain to show what is taking place behind the stage of world history. One problem we face today is that we have become so secular it is hard for us to understand and perceive that reality doesn't end with those things we can see and measure. The universe contains spiritual forces that impact the material universe. The Bible provides great insight into these spiritual forces and explains that they are a created order of beings called angels. Angels are not the immaterial spirits of humans who have died. They are nonhuman, spiritual beings created by God before He formed the earth.

These spiritual beings fall into two classes—angels and demons. Angels are those beings who, after their creation, remained true to God. Demons are spirit beings who were created perfect but who chose to rebel against their Creator. They followed another created angelic being who led this revolt against God. That spirit being has several names: "The great dragon was hurled down—that ancient serpent called the devil, or Satan, who leads the whole world astray" (Revelation 12:9). From the time of his fall, Satan opposed God and His plans. He enticed Adam and Eve to sin by eating the forbidden fruit (Genesis

3:1-7). He accused Job (Job 1:6-12; 2:1-7) and the high priest Joshua (Zechariah 3:1-2) before God.

Satan has worked throughout history to oppose God's plans and His people. The Apostle John zeros in on two specific incidents that show the extent to which Satan will go to oppose God. John begins Revelation 12 by painting a picture of "a woman clothed with the sun, with the moon under her feet and a crown of twelve stars on her head" (v. 1). John borrows this image from Joseph's dream in Genesis 37, in which "the sun and moon and eleven stars were bowing down" to Joseph (v. 9). In the very next verse Joseph's father, Israel, explains the verse. He is the sun, his wife is the moon, and Joseph's eleven brothers are the stars. In the Apostle John's vision the woman clothed with the sun, the moon, and the twelve stars represents the nation of Israel.

John continues in his vision by explaining that Israel is about to give birth to a child—"a son, a male child, who will rule all the nations with an iron scepter" (Revelation 12:5). This child symbolizes Jesus Christ, the Messiah God promised to the nation of Israel. God also announced that He would rule the world. But Satan seeks to pervert God's plan: "The dragon stood in front of the woman who was about to give birth, so that he might devour her child the moment it was born" (12:4). Satan tried to short-circuit God's plans for the earth by eliminating God's Messiah.

Satan's fingerprints are on all the opposition and hatred directed against Jesus Christ when He was here on earth. At the time of Jesus' birth, Herod the Great gave orders to kill all the boys of Bethlehem who were two years old and under (Matthew 2:7-8, 16-18). Just after His baptism Satan tried to seduce Him in the wilderness with the lust of the flesh, the lust of the eyes, and the pride of life (4:1-11). Satan used Peter, one of Jesus' most trusted disciples, to try to turn Jesus from His intended task (16:21-23). Satan entered the heart of Judas to betray Jesus (John 13:21-30). No doubt Satan whispered in the ears of those shouting for Jesus' crucifixion.

If Satan thought he had foiled God's program by killing His Son, then Satan was sorely disappointed when, on the third day, Jesus rose from the dead: "And her child was snatched up to God and to his throne" (Revelation 12:5). Satan had not factored in Jesus' resurrection from the dead in his plans. But when Plan A had failed, Satan turned to Plan B. If he could not destroy God's Messiah, then he would try to destroy the Jewish people over whom the Messiah was to rule.

Satan promotes much anti-Semitic activity today. He hates God, and he vents his hatred on the people chosen by God. Spiritual forces are at work to turn the world against the Jews. We must be sensitive to those forces at work around us, and we must pray for the Jews and for the nation of Israel.

Trouble on the Horizon

After describing the satanic attack on the Messiah, the Apostle John details Satan's coming attack against the nation of Israel. John begins by describing God's protection of His people: "The woman fled into the desert to a place prepared for her by God, where she might be taken care of for 1,260 days" (Revelation 12:6). We examined this three-and-a-half-year period in chapter 5. It refers to the last half of the seven-year period still to come on the earth.

John explains why the nation of Israel will need a place to hide for this final period of time. He describes an awesome battle in heaven between the forces of God, led by Michael, and the forces of Satan. Satan will finally and permanently be barred from heaven. When he realizes the end is near, Satan redoubles his effort to destroy the people of God. "When the dragon saw that he had been hurled to the earth, he pursued the woman who had given birth to the male child" (12:13).

John describes a final three-and-a-half-year period when the Jews and the nation of Israel will be the special target of satanic attack and opposition. This attack precedes Jesus' return to earth to set up His kingdom. John provides much detail about this coming time of persecution, but he is not the only prophet to predict the anti-Semitic activity that will characterize the end times.

Daniel described the end-time troubles that Israel would face. In Daniel 7 he described a fourth and final empire that would rule the earth just before the coming of God's kingdom. The leader would exalt himself above God and would attempt to destroy the nation of Israel. "He will speak against the Most High and oppress his saints and try to change the set times and the laws. The saints will be handed over to him for a time, times and half a time" (Daniel 7:25). Later Daniel described this end-time period as a time of spiritual warfare and physical persecution:

> At that time Michael, the great prince who protects your people, will arise. There will be a time of distress such as has not happened from the beginning of nations until then. But at that time your people—everyone whose name is found written in the book—will be delivered. (Daniel 12:1)

Michael, the same archangel named by the Apostle John, will lead the spiritual forces fighting for Israel against Satan.

Perhaps the most frightening detail provided by Daniel is the severity of the persecution Israel will experience during these final days. As awful as the atrocities committed by Hitler and his evil empire were, the actions of the end-time ruler will be more severe.

The prophet Jeremiah also wrote that a time of unparalleled trouble would engulf the Jews just before the establishment of their kingdom. In Jeremiah 30–33 the prophet penned his words of future comfort to a nation about to be carried away to exile in Babylon. He began by announcing God's ultimate restoration of all Jews in the final days: "'The days are coming,' declares the LORD, 'when I will bring my people Israel and Judah back from captivity and restore them to the land I gave their forefathers to possess,' says the LORD" (30:3). But before that day could dawn a time of trouble would descend on the nation. "How awful

that day will be! None will be like it. It will be a time
of trouble for Jacob, but he will be saved out of it"
(30:7).

Nearly six centuries after Daniel and Jeremiah,
Jesus described this same time of trouble to His disciples. Jesus traced the end-time events up to the middle
of the seven-year period when the "abomination of
desolation spoken of through the prophet Daniel"
would be set up in the temple. That act is the signal
for the Jews to flee for their lives. "For then there will
be great distress, unequaled from the beginning of the
world until now—and never to be equaled again. If
those days had not been cut short, no one would survive, but for the sake of the elect those days will be
shortened" (Matthew 24:21-22). This time of terror
ends when the world awakes to "see the Son of Man
coming on the clouds of the sky, with power and great
glory" (24:30). This unique period of persecution is
cut short by the return of Jesus Christ to earth.

Prophecy or Prejudice?

All the prophets above seem to describe a time of terrible suffering still ahead for the nation of Israel. But is
there not a danger that by announcing such a thing we
could be promoting anti-Semitism? That is, might we
so eagerly desire the end-time events to come that we
unconsciously allow, encourage, or promote anti-
Semitic activities to hasten along God's prophecies?

Such an attitude is possible, but it is not biblical.
God may have told us what will happen in the future,
but He has not told us when those events will take
place. A true believer in Jesus today must be com-

pelled by three specific convictions. First, the task God has assigned to us in this age is to tell others about the good news of eternal life that can be found only in Jesus Christ. God called us to be witnesses for Jesus Christ, not date-setters (see Acts 1:6-8). Second, we are to be characterized by love for others, and this must include Jews (John 13:34; 1 Corinthians 13:1-13; Galatians 5:22). Third, we need to remember that God will curse those who curse the descendants of Abraham (Genesis 12:3). Those who encourage, promote, or participate in anti-Semitic activities are attacking God's chosen people and will be cursed by God.

The words Jesus used to describe His own betrayal by Judas can be applied to all who raise their fists in anger against the Jews. Though it might even be part of God's eternal plan (as was the death of Jesus), God will still hold responsible all who participate in such evil. "The Son of Man will go [to his death] just as it is written about him. But woe to that man who betrays the Son of Man! It would be better for him if he had not been born" (Mark 14:21). To be anti-Semitic is to oppose the plan of God.

PART TWO

THE MIDDLE EAST: OIL, ISLAM, AND THE NEW NEBUCHADNEZZAR

While growing up in rural Pennsylvania, I worked for a time in a local dairy. The farmer for whom I worked processed and sold his milk at a store on his property. Two friends and I processed, bottled, and hauled the milk from the dairy to the store. I was sixteen years old—and I was also the oldest of the three student employees! We worked hard, but we also managed to have some fun. As part of the cleaning routine we had to flush out the pipes with a lye solution. We also used a weak acid for cleaning and purging the equipment. Having studied high-school chemistry, we understood the basics of not mixing an acid and a base (such as lye) together. But our curiosity of what would really happen overcame our common sense, and we decided to try an experiment. We filled a glass milk bottle half full with the lye solution. We then set it on the floor and poured in the weak acid solution.

The resulting chemical reaction heated the bottle and produced a boiling, seething liquid that exploded out the top of the bottle. We scrambled for cover behind the stainless-steel holding tanks until the reaction stopped. We saw firsthand that mixing such volatile elements can result in a violent explosion.

The Volatile Middle East

The Middle East is as volatile a mixture geographically and ethnically as that "milk-bottle bomb" my friends and I prepared in the dairy. Ethnic violence and religious hatred abound in the Middle East. The Arabs and the Jews do not like each other. The Arab Sunni Muslim majority clashes with the Persian Shiite Muslim minority. The Kurds alternately fight the

Turks, the Syrians, the Iranians, and the Iraqis to regain a national homeland. The Arabs clamor for unity, but they cannot agree who should lead this united Arab nation. Each of these events has the potential to spark another Middle East conflict. The recipe for international conflict focuses on events in the Middle East.

Recipe for Middle East Turmoil

- Take one land (Israel) and try to divide it into two equal parts. Set aside the section labeled "to the Arabs," but don't do anything with it yet.
- Add in the growth of radical Shiite-Muslim extremism and ultra-Orthodox Jewish nationalism.
- Add a pinch of Saddam Hussein, Muammar Qaddafi, and Arab terrorism.
- Add one disintegrating former-Communist state and the possible proliferation of nuclear technology.
- Mix well and let simmer until it explodes.

How do the tremendous changes in the entire Middle East fit into God's prophetic puzzle? Can we discern a pattern emerging that might point toward God's future program for the Middle East? How do Russia, Iraq, Iran, Turkey, or Libya fit into God's prophetic program? These are the questions we will explore in this section.

During the fall of 1990 and spring of 1991 the

world focused on events in the Middle East. Prophecy seemed to be coming true right before our eyes. But then the coalition forces defeated Saddam Hussein. Fears of a collapsing world economy crowded out interest in Bible prophecy and the Middle East. Saddam seemed "on the ropes," and his vaunted army was in tatters. Was Operation Desert Storm part of Bible prophecy after all?

In this section we will take a fresh look at current events in the Middle East in light of Bible prophecy. Spread out your maps of the Middle East and open your Bible as we put the pieces of God's prophetic puzzle in order.

CHAPTER SEVEN
RUSSIA: HAS THE BEAR BEEN DECLAWED?

Growing up in the dark days of the Cold War, my first memories of the Soviet Union are images of a larger-than-life Evil Empire watching for ways to burn the United States into a nuclear cinder. The Soviets launched *Sputnik* when I was seven years old, but our teachers did not hail the event as a milestone in humanity's efforts to explore the heavens. Instead, they taught us the fear of nuclear warheads plummeting from the sky. During the Cuban Missile Crisis in 1962 our family drove to a nearby town to view fallout shelters on display. We had to be ever vigilant lest the evil Communists swoop down on us by surprise.

As recently as the early 1980s the United States still felt locked in a mortal struggle with the Soviet Union. The Reagan administration invested billions of dollars developing a "Star Wars" defensive umbrella to protect against nuclear attack. But along the way something happened. While the United States continued arming itself to be ready for the inevitable Soviet attack, the Soviet Union

collapsed and died. Its obituary appeared in the world
press Thursday, December 26, 1991:

> Conceived in utopian promise and born in the
> violent upheavals of the "Great October Revolu-
> tion of 1917," the union heaved its last breath in
> the dreary darkness of late December 1991,
> stripped of ideology, dismembered, bankrupt and
> hungry—but awe-inspiring even in its fall.
>   The end came with the resignation of President
> Mikhail Gorbachev to make way for a new
> "Commonwealth of Independent States."[1]

Will the Bear Be Back?

Does the collapse of the Soviet Union mean the end of
Russian influence in the world? Not by any stretch of
the imagination! The old Soviet nuclear arsenal, even
with its planned reductions, will still rival that of any
nuclear power in the world. Its land and naval forces
remain strong. The Republic of Russia dominated the
old Soviet Union, and it will dominate the new Commonwealth.

The old Communist system of government might
be dead, but the land in which it once lived is still very
much alive. The country boasts great natural resources
and a vast pool of well-educated engineers and scientists who have designed and manufactured some of
the most terrifying military equipment and instru-
ments of mass destruction. Russia still has the basic
resources to rebuild her tattered economy—if she can
repair her inefficient system of transportation and distribution and rebuild her dilapidated infrastructure.

Will the End of Communism Bring Peace?

The world will be a more peaceful and prosperous place in the 1990s than it has been in the decades since World War II because the premises by which it is governed have changed. In the coming years it will no longer be ruled to suit the needs of ideological and military competition, but instead to promote international trade and the well-being of the trading nations. Major military conflicts will be all but unthinkable because they are contrary to the mutual interests of the trading nations.[2]

Thus, as we come to the last decade of this millennium, we find democracy has emerged as the triumphant and preferred ideology of the whole world, while dictatorial ideologies both of the left and of the right have fallen into disrepute. One can only hope this will be irreversible.[3]

You will hear of wars and rumors of wars, but see to it that you are not alarmed. Such things must happen, but the end is still to come. Nation will rise against nation, and kingdom against kingdom. (Matthew 24:6-7)

The early 1990s witnessed the rapid collapse of totalitarian governments and dictators. The death of the Soviet Union was especially significant because it was the fountainhead of Communistic government. From its beginnings in 1917, the Soviet Union dedicated itself to exporting its brand of totalitarian government around the world. The bankruptcy of Communism in the Soviet Union—a large country with tremendous resources—sent shock waves around the world. But will peace follow?

If Yugoslavia is any indication, the answer might be no. One benefit of a strong central government in the Soviet Union and her allies was to hold in check ethnic and religious rivalries. The rivalries still existed, but the government clamped a lid on dissent, producing a pressure-cooker environment where hatreds and fears grew in intensity. When the lid came off, the hatreds and rivalries exploded.

As the world celebrates the collapse of Communism, a new danger looms on the horizon. It's a danger unseen in the world since the end of World War II—rising nationalism. A few snapshots raise unsettling images from days gone by.

Snapshot #1: Germany. In the summer of 1990, East and West Germany reunited. The new country—80 million strong—instantly became the economic powerhouse of Europe. The reunification led to a surge of German nationalism—and violence. In 1991 Germany experienced more racial attacks than at any time since the early Nazi years.[4] The number of attacks surged to almost 2,000 in 1992. A recent poll found that almost two-thirds of all Germans "don't trust themselves to express their true opinion about Jews."[5] The most frightening trend is the rise in neo-Nazi sympathizers among fifteen- to twenty-five-year-old men.

Snapshot #2: Yugoslavia. The collapse of Communism reignited sectarian violence among the Croats and Serbs. Fourteen cease-fire agreements were made—and broken—during 1991. The fighting claimed 5,000 lives and produced more than 500,000 refugees. The fighting intensified in 1992, and the world seemed powerless to put an end to the conflict. With their economy in shambles, the people of Yugoslavia wait for the United Nations, the European Economic Community, or another strong outside power to impose peace. The violence is a deadly replay of the ethnic warfare that consumed the land earlier in the century.

Snapshot #3: Armenia and Azerbaijan. Ethnic violence between Christian Armenians and Muslim Azerbaijanis flared up in 1988. Since then hundreds have died. Moscow sent troops to maintain order. But with the collapse of the Soviet Union's strong central government, the violence has escalated. The president of Azerbaijan states the problem concisely: "We are at war with Armenia."

Communism collapsed in Russia, but, if democracy cannot put food on the tables, it will suffer a similar fate. Americans cheered the thousands of Russians who stood with Boris Yeltsin during the ill-fated Communist coup in August 1991. But relatively few Russians joined in the protest. Most were too busy waiting in line for food to care what was happening with their government. The dramatic rise in food prices under the new democracy has already produced mass protests. Thousands have taken to the streets demanding a return to the "good old days"—when Stalin ruled the Soviet Union!

The end of Communism will not bring peace because the real enemy of world peace is not a system but sin. The world longs for peace, but true peace will only come when the Prince of Peace returns to earth. The collapse of the Soviet Union will not bring world peace, nor will it eliminate the problems facing those standing in breadlines in Moscow. The world will continue to struggle because the essential problems remain unchanged.

> Finally, at this coming turn of the century, mankind is overwhelmed by the scope of the phenomena coming at it from all sides, overwhelmed—and the word is not too strong—because the traditional structures, governments and institutions can no longer manage the problem in their present dimension. To make things worse, the archaic and unsuitable structures are set in a true moral crisis. The disappearance of value systems, the questioning of traditions, the collapse of ideologies, the absence of a global vision, the limits of the current practices of democracy confirm the void confronting societies.[6]

Today Christians are to promote righteousness and justice in the world. We can—and should—make a difference in society as we seek to be salt and light in a corrupt and dark age. As long as we are here on earth, it is our obligation to display the character of God's future kingdom in our lives. God has predicted that lasting peace will not come to the world until Jesus returns to set up His kingdom. But Christians cannot use this as an excuse just to give up and not try to change the world today. The root cause of the world's ills is sin, and God has given us the message that can make a difference.

Is Russia in Bible Prophecy?

The world watched in awe at the sudden, dramatic decline of the Soviet Union. While some are still skeptical of a Communist hoax to lull the West into disarmament, most believe a profound change occurred in Russia and the other republics. But what does this mean for Bible prophecy? Does the Bible predict an end-time Russia reasserting its ruthless goals to dominate the Middle East, or is Russia absent from the pages of prophecy?

The one central passage where many scholars see Russia in Bible prophecy is Ezekiel 38–39. In these chapters Ezekiel predicts that a confederation of forces led by a leader named Gog will invade Israel. Who is this man with the funny name, and what countries are coming with him against Israel? Why do some see Russia in this prediction?

God commanded Ezekiel to prophesy against "Gog, of the land of Magog, the chief prince of Meshech and Tubal" (38:2). Though it may not be apparent at first, some see in this verse a veiled reference to Russia. First, the word *chief* is the Hebrew word *rosh,* which is the Hebrew word for *head.* The word can be used as either a noun or an adjective. Without being too technical, we do the same thing with the English word *head.* We place a hat on our head (used as a noun), but in a restaurant we will consult the head waiter (used as an adjective). The English quotation I used above translated *rosh* as an adjective, calling Gog the *chief* prince. However, others believe that *rosh* should be translated as a noun. In this translation Gog is the "prince of Rosh." And where is Rosh? Many believe it is the land later called Russia.

Second, some see Russia in Ezekiel 38 because of the other names Ezekiel used in this passage. If *Rosh* is Russia, then could not *Meshech* be Moscow and *Tubal* be Tobolsk, located east of the Ural Mountains? These cities are in Russia, and some believe the modern cities preserve the names found in Ezekiel.

Third, some see Russia in Ezekiel 38 because of the similarity between Russia and other descriptions of this invading nation found in Ezekiel 38–39. Ezekiel described an invincible army with many allies descending on Israel. Certainly Russia has a large army with many allies from the former Warsaw-Pact nations. Ezekiel also said the army would come "from the far north" (38:6), and Russia is the nation to the far north above Israel. These parallels have convinced some that Ezekiel was predicting an invasion by Russia.

How do we approach a passage as complicated as Ezekiel 38–39? The key point in interpreting Ezekiel's prophecy is to identify the nations named by Ezekiel. Where were these countries in Ezekiel's day? Was *rosh* a country, or did Ezekiel use the word as an adjective? We need to interpret the Bible before we look at current events.

The countries named by Ezekiel existed in his day.

In fact, Moses identified many of the countries nearly 900 years before Ezekiel when he explained to Israel how all nations descended from the sons of Noah. Comparing Moses' list in Genesis 10:2-5 with Ezekiel's list shows many similarities. Both name the nations of Magog, Meshech, Tubal, Gomer, and Togarmah. But the Genesis account knows of no nation named Rosh. Most likely, therefore, Ezekiel used the name as an adjective to describe this leader. He will be the "head prince" of these other countries.

Much work has been done on identifying the other countries named by Moses and Ezekiel. Gomer appears in Assyrian writings as Gimirrai and in Greek writings as Kimmérioi.[7] These people, also called the Cimmerians, lived in eastern Asia Minor near Armenia. Magog was the father of the Scythian peoples who lived between the Black and Caspian seas. These nations lived in what is today eastern Turkey, Armenia, Azerbaijan, Georgia, and the very southern tip of Russia.

The Bible always associates Meshech and Tubal together. Before Ezekiel's time the Assyrians mentioned the land of Tabal(u) next to the land of Musku. Some scholars place these groups in what is today eastern Turkey. "Their movement was from eastern Asia Minor north to the Black Sea."[8] Togarmah is the remaining group mentioned by Ezekiel. In Genesis 10 Moses explained that Togarmah descended from Gomer. Ancient writings from 700 years before Ezekiel mention a district and city of Tagarma, north of the road from Haran to Carchemish.[9] This would place Togarmah in eastern Turkey.

Where were the countries identified by Ezekiel in chapter 38? The countries controlled the rugged area north and east of the Fertile Crescent in what is today northern and eastern Turkey, northwestern Iran, and the former Soviet republics of Georgia, Armenia, and Azerbaijan. Only a small sliver of what is today Russia lies within the area named by Ezekiel. We should interpret Ezekiel 38 by identifying the areas named by Ezekiel instead of trying to find modern names that sound similar to those in the passage. Ezekiel predicts an attack against Israel that will come from the region of Turkey, and the area between the Black and Caspian seas. Russia proper is not named by Ezekiel.

Ezekiel predicted that the countries in this geographical area would ally themselves with others in an attack against Israel. The former Soviet Union could have been part of the alliance because she controlled the area between the Black and Caspian seas. The current Commonwealth of Independent States also could be part of the alliance because it includes the area between the Black and Caspian seas. However, it is just as likely that the individual republics could break away from the Commonwealth and act on their own.

So what is the final answer? Is Russia in Bible prophecy? Based on my understanding of Ezekiel 38, I would say the answer at the present time is probably no. Ezekiel does not seem to name Russia in his prophecy, and the lands that he says will attack Israel do not include Russia. Russia would only become part of Ezekiel's prophecy if she would again exert control over those lands between the Black and Caspian seas. Events are changing rapidly in that part of the world, and the final boundaries are not yet drawn. Ezekiel tells us where the attack will originate, but he does not say what nations will control the area and unleash the attack.

Russia might play a role in end-time events, but she will not play a major part. Even if Russia is included in the prophecy of Ezekiel 38–39, the battle occupies only a small place in God's overall drama. In chapter 11 we will look more closely at the battle of Ezekiel 38–39 and try to determine when the battle will take place and who will participate. We only examined part of the roster of rebellious nations in this chapter. Still others will unite in this criminal conspiracy against Israel.

C H A P T E R   E I G H T
OIL: THE ACHILLES' HEEL OF WESTERN CIVILIZATION

The world is addicted to fossil fuels. Low-cost oil and
natural gas spin the turbines, heat the homes, and
power the vehicles that define Western civilization.
The magic elixir from the bowels of the earth transformed society—but at a price. Events as unrelated as
the grounding of the *Exxon Valdez* and Operation Desert Storm have one common denominator—oil. Oil
drives our economy:

> The belief that monetary management or even
> manipulation can lead to a proper accounting and
> evaluation of growth and development needs to
> be eradicated. Energy, on the other hand, is the
> driving force in the economy; money is simply
> its surrogate. There is surely a strong argument at
> this stage of human development to devise a new
> economics based on the flow of energy.[1]

If energy is the currency of the 1990s, then oil is the
"gold standard" and the Middle East is the mother
lode. Fifty percent of the world's proven oil reserves

remain locked under the sands surrounding the Persian Gulf. Saudi Arabia alone accounts for 25 percent of the world's proven oil reserves, and Kuwait and Iraq account for another 25 percent. The Middle East is known for two things—oil and instability.

Western civilization's reliance on oil became painfully clear in 1973. When the United States decided to help resupply Israel during the Yom Kippur War, the Muslim countries retaliated by reducing oil production and banning oil sales to the United States. Overnight the price of oil quadrupled. Millions of Americans spent their days stuck in gas lines at service stations. The embargo finally ended, but oil prices continued to rise. By the end of the 1970s the price of a barrel of oil had increased tenfold over its pre-1973 price.

The Failure of Oil Independence

The dramatic rise in oil prices sparked a wave of oil exploration and energy conservation. The gas-guzzling road cruisers of the early 1970s belched their way into extinction as fuel-efficient subcompact cars rolled off the assembly lines and into the driveways of American homes. The price of oil also made exploration in remote regions of the world economically viable. By 1975 oil flowed from the rough waters of the North Sea. By 1977 it snaked down a pipeline from Alaska's Prudhoe Bay to the port of Valdez. Europe and the United States began to wean themselves from excessive dependence on Middle-Eastern oil.

Besides oil exploration and energy conservation, the West also embraced alternative sources of energy—especially nuclear power. Europe accelerated its program to provide low-cost nuclear power, and by the end of 1980 half of the world's nuclear reactors were in Europe. The United States also expanded its reliance on nuclear energy—though opposition from environmental groups slowed construction of many reactors. Still, many hailed nuclear power as one solution to dependence on foreign oil.

Two major events in the 1980s undid many of the West's efforts to break free of its dependence on foreign oil. First, increased exploration produced a glut in world oil supplies and a dramatic decline in oil prices. The oil glut shattered the power of the OPEC cartel, but it also derailed many efforts to wean the West off imported oil. Companies abandoned research on exotic—and expensive—alternatives to oil, and oil exploration slowed. When the price of crude oil dipped below $20 per barrel, it became cheaper to import foreign oil than to develop domestic sources. The West's dependence on foreign oil again began to increase.

The second setback in the 1980s was the heightened fear over nuclear power as a safe, economical energy alternative. On March 28, 1979, the name *Three Mile Island* vaulted from obscurity to shake our nation's faith in the safety of nuclear energy. A near-meltdown at the number-two reactor released radioactivity into the atmosphere near Harrisburg, Pennsylvania. The nation came perilously close to suffering its first major nuclear catastrophe. Three Mile Island became a symbol of the malevolent nuclear

genie waiting to be released through human or
mechanical error.

Seven years later the genie burst his bonds in the
Soviet Union. On April 26, 1986, the Chernobyl
nuclear plant suffered a catastrophic explosion.
Nuclear debris shot into the air and rained down
throughout Europe. The Soviet government relocated
those who lived in the region around Chernobyl, but
the move came too late for many. By most estimates
the final death toll from radiation-induced cancer will
reach into the tens of thousands. The Chernobyl disaster cast a dark shadow over the future of nuclear
power.

Cheap oil and the threat of a nuclear catastrophe
doomed the West's efforts to break their addiction to
foreign oil. Eight days before the Chernobyl disaster
the U.S. Synthetic Fuels Corporation, established by
Congress in 1980, officially went out of business. The
decline in oil prices made the grand scheme too expensive to continue.

Operation Desert Storm

As the 1990s began, the West's dependence on foreign oil continued to increase. The United States now
receives nearly one quarter of its oil from the Middle
East. Saddam Hussein illustrated the frailty of dependence on Middle East oil when he invaded Kuwait in
August 1990. In twenty-four hours he went from controlling 12 percent of the world's proven oil reserves
to controlling 25 percent of those reserves. Even more
frightening was the possibility that he would not stop
at Kuwait but would continue into Saudi Arabia. That

fear sent the world price of oil skyrocketing from $16 per barrel in July 1990 to a peak of $42 per barrel in October.

Allied intervention spared Saudi Arabia and rescued Kuwait. But above all, Operation Desert Storm protected the West's oil supplies. And yet, did we learn the lesson of how vulnerable we are because of our dependence on foreign oil? The answer is no! Before the fighting even stopped, the price of oil dropped back to prewar levels. Oil exploration, which enjoyed a brief renaissance during the months following the invasion of Kuwait, declined rapidly as the price of foreign oil dropped. The West suffered a momentary scare, but soon forgot why.

The United States underwent a rapid shift in emotions following Operation Desert Storm. When the war ended, the Allied forces basked in the glow of victory. We had smashed Saddam Hussein's army and liberated Kuwait. The technical superiority of our weapons eclipsed even our wildest expectations. The national anxiety that had plagued us since Vietnam was replaced with old-fashioned, flag-waving patriotism.

Our first flush of victory was followed by a deep desire for peace. Saddam Hussein was on the ropes, and we expected him to be eliminated soon. The possibility of peace between Israel and her neighbors seemed believable, if not inevitable. The summer of 1991 brought great predictions of a New World Order that would transform the Middle East as it had been transforming Eastern Europe and the Soviet Union.

Unfortunately, hope soon gave way to pessimism

and despair. Saddam Hussein was the villain who
would not go away. The Middle East peace talks
slowed to a glacial pace as the different groups wran-
gled over the tiniest procedural details. The economic
bills of Operation Desert Storm came due, and the
United States found itself strapped for cash. Military
cutbacks and a deepening recession made many
Americans realize the enormous cost associated with
leading the free world. Hussein took a backseat to
health care as America became obsessed with its own
problems. Had anything really changed?

> What then are the energy prospects? While there
> is a present glut of oil, we are nearing the end of
> the long period during which this nonrenewable
> resource has been cheap and plentiful.[2]

Oil and the End Times

Does oil enter God's plans for the end times? This
question must be approached two ways. First, we
must see if the Bible provides any direct references to
oil in God's prophetic plans. Second, we must examine any indirect references or allusions that might
relate to oil.

Some Bible students point to Deuteronomy 33 and
see a prediction of oil coming from the land of Israel:
"About Asher he said: 'Most blessed of sons is Asher;
let him be favored by his brothers, and let him bathe
his feet in oil'" (Deuteronomy 33:24). Some individuals have attempted to drill for oil in northern Israel
because of this verse. But those who see petroleum in
Deuteronomy 33 are mistaken. The "oil" predicted by

Moses is olive oil, not petroleum. Moses, like the patriarch Jacob, predicted that Asher would experience a good life from bountiful produce (see Genesis 49:20).

The only direct reference to the petroleum products of the Middle East comes from the book of Genesis. When describing the building of the Tower of Babel, Moses reported that the workers "used brick instead of stone, and tar for mortar" (11:3). Builders in ancient Mesopotamia used a thick, tarlike petroleum substance as a form of mortar. In the ancient Near East, petroleum was more important for building than for burning.

No specific Bible prophecies ever predict that oil will play a major role in end-time events. Thus we must be careful lest we misuse God's Word. But are there any indirect passages that can help us decide if oil might play a major role in the end times? I believe the Bible does describe some end-time activities that might point to the importance of oil.

First, the Bible predicts the rise of Babylon in the end times. I examined this at some length in *The Rise of Babylon,* and I will come back to it in chapter 10. But stated briefly, the Bible predicts that the literal city of Babylon will be rebuilt and will play an important role in end-time events. The book of Revelation describes the city as a center of incredible wealth where "the merchants of the earth grew rich from her excessive luxuries" (Revelation 18:3). John records a sample list of the luxury items these merchants sold to the city in verses 12-13. He also reports that "every sea captain, and all who travel by ship, the sailors, and all who earn their living from the sea" (v. 17) will mourn the fall of this city. They are sad because "all who had ships on the sea became rich through her wealth" but now "in one hour she has been brought to ruin" (18:17-19).

The Bible predicts that Babylon, in southern Iraq, will reach a position of worldwide influence and power in the final days. She will have money to spend on luxury items from around the world, and the world's merchants and traders will live well catering to her needs. But John's description does not match with our understanding of present-day Babylon. Wasn't Iraq bombed out of the twentieth century? Wasn't that nation crippled so much that she could never recover to the level described in the Bible?

As it turns out, we overestimated our early assessment of Iraq's damage. We destroyed much of Saddam Hussein's army, but much remains. We destroyed much of his weapons-manufacturing capabilities, but he is still playing a shell game with United Nations inspectors who are searching for his hidden nuclear and chemical weapons facilities. His regime did not collapse as we had hoped. In fact, in an ironic twist of fate, Saddam Hussein stayed in power while George Bush was voted out of office. Iraq may be down, but she is not out.

Could Iraq make a quick comeback? Yes she could, if the United States were not watching Saddam Hussein's every move. He still has enough military might to retake Kuwait, should he so desire. And without America's assistance, Saudi Arabia also would be vulnerable. If Saddam Hussein or a successor could gain control of 50 percent of the world's proven oil reserves, then he could quickly gain the worldwide wealth and power described in the Bible. In fact, it seems that this could only happen through the control of Middle-East oil. Though the Bible may not mention oil specifically, from what we know today it seems likely that oil will be the vehicle used by Babylon to gain worldwide wealth and power.

God placed the world's resources according to divine wisdom, and He is working in history to accomplish His sovereign plan. God predicts that the end times will revolve around events in the Middle East. He also placed in the Middle East the one resource on which the world is so dependent. Coincidence? Perhaps. But it seems more likely that the world's dependence on oil at this time in human history is no accident. As the end times loom ever closer, we find ourselves watching events unfold in the Middle East. The politics of oil coincide with the prophecies of old.

C H A P T E R   N I N E
ISLAM AND THE MYTH OF ARAB UNITY

Iraq also considers that, despite all that the Arab
nation suffered during the Ottoman period, then under
the yoke of Western colonialism, in terms of contempt, divisions, repression, and attempts to distort
identity, the components of its unity have remained
solid and alive. Despite its division into states, the
Arab world nevertheless remains one country, every
inch of which must be considered in accordance with
a nationalistic vision and, more particularly, in accordance with the demands of a common Arab national
security. We must avoid falling into a narrow and self-
ish point of view when considering the interests and
rights of this or that country. The higher interests of
the Arab nation as well as the strategic calculations
essential to Arab national security must be ever present in our minds and must be paramount in inter-Arab
relations.[1]

Two weeks after Tariq Aziz, Iraq's minister of foreign affairs, delivered this impassioned plea for Arab
unity and security, Iraq's tanks and armored vehicles
rumbled across the border into Kuwait. On August 2,

1990, Iraq's invasion of her helpless neighbor shattered the myth of Arab unity. The condemnation and armed conflict that followed pitted Arab against Arab and forced several Islamic countries to side with the "infidels" from the West against their Muslim brothers. What happened to Arab unity?

The Myth of Arab Unity

America's perception of the Middle East is a kaleidoscope of generalizations, misinformation, prejudice, and paranoia. In a geography survey done several years ago, most participants could not correctly identify the Persian Gulf. (The Gulf War has helped our knowledge of geography!) Ask the average American to describe the people of the Middle East, and he or she will tell you that they are:

- Arab by nationality
- Muslim by faith
- Wealthy because of oil
- Primitive in technological sophistication
- Fanatical in their hatred of Americans

Every one of these descriptions is incorrect! America's view of the Middle East comes mostly from "Headline News" and Hollywood. As a result, most Americans have a simplistic, distorted picture of the people who live in the Middle East.

Not All Are Arabs

Not everyone in the Middle East is Arab. By definition an Arab is an individual who speaks Arabic and who identifies with the Arab culture. Turkey is Muslim in religion, but the people speak Turkish, not Arabic. The vast majority of the population in Iran are Persians, not Arabs. They speak Farsi instead of Arabic. The Kurdish people living in Turkey, Syria, Iraq, and Iran speak Kurdish and are fighting each country to gain autonomy.

Even in those countries usually identified as Arab, vast differences exist. The people of Egypt are proud of their ancient culture and heritage. They are not just Arabs, they are Egyptians. The same feeling of nationalism is true of Jordanians, Palestinians, Kuwaitis, and Syrians. They speak the same language, but they also have distinct cultural and historical traditions that set them apart.

Not All Are Muslims

Most inhabitants in the Middle East follow the Muslim faith, but many Americans do not realize that religious differences do exist in the Middle East. For example, large numbers of Arabs do claim to be Christians—mostly followers of the Catholic and Orthodox faiths. In Egypt over 17 percent of the population calls itself Christian. The number rises to 30 percent in Lebanon. A larger percentage of Christians live in Iraq and Kuwait than in Israel.[2]

Even those who call themselves Muslims are not united. The Muslim faith is not a single, monolithic unity. Two main branches arose within Islam. The Sunni branch is the main branch and claims to follow the traditional Way (sunna) of the prophet Muhammad. Soon after Muhammad died, his followers split.

One group, called the Shiites, rejected the leaders who followed Muhammad. Instead they recognized Muhammad's son-in-law, Ali, and his descendants as the rightful successors to Muhammad. The Shiites live mainly in southern Iraq and in Iran.

Not All Are Wealthy

Perhaps the most common perception among Americans is that all Arabs are wealthy. More than 170 million Arabs live in the Middle East. Of this number only 10 percent live in countries that are considered wealthy by Western standards. The rest live in less fortunate countries struggling with large populations and poor natural resources. Many resent the lavish displays of wealth by their rich Muslim neighbors and the contempt with which they are treated by those countries that have such abundance.

Saddam Hussein struck a responsive cord in the hearts of many Arabs when he painted himself as the Savior of the masses:

> Finally, for the first time since Egypt's Gamal Shawki Abdel Nasser, an Arab leader had been bold enough to stand up to the West and had said all the catchwords—Palestine, Islam, unity, sharing Arab oil—that reminded the Arabs how much should be right and how much had gone wrong.[3]

Americans shook their heads as Palestinians and Jordanians marched in support of Saddam Hussein. How could anyone follow this dictator? We didn't

listen as he spoke the words these oppressed people
wanted to hear. The Kuwaitis had only offered menial
jobs and minuscule financial assistance. Hussein
offered the Arab masses pride and hope for a future.

Not All Are Technologically Unsophisticated

The Iraqi army crumbled under the relentless bombing
and "Hail Mary" tank offensive in Operation Desert
Storm. The ease with which the Allies gained air superiority and smashed through Iraqi defensive positions
confirmed our belief that the war was a mismatch.
The unsophisticated Iraqi soldiers were no match for
the West's high-tech arsenal.

Only after the war did the West get a glimpse at just
how sophisticated Iraq had become. When the war
began, experts predicted that Saddam's nuclear arsenal could be operational in five years. After the war
those same experts traveled to Iraq to view bomb damage and examine secret files. They have yet to ferret
out all of Saddam Hussein's secrets. But based on the
evidence uncovered so far, they believe Iraq was on
the threshold of producing nuclear weapons. Hussein
had already produced large quantities of chemical and
biological weapons. The inspectors also uncovered
plans and materials for building "superguns" to launch
these destructive payloads hundreds of miles. How
had we so underestimated Iraq's capabilities?

The West seems consistently to underestimate the
intellectual sophistication of the Middle East. We
watch news stories of fanatical suicide bombers in
Lebanon or camel-riding bedouin in Saudi Arabia,
and we naively believe that all Arabs must live and act

the same way. Most don't understand or appreciate the long cultural and scientific heritage in Islam.

While Europe groped its way through the Dark Ages, Arab scholars continued the scientific progress begun by the Greeks and Romans: "The Arabs not only preserved, refined, updated and translated into Arabic the rich heritage of classical Greek knowledge, but they also added original and significant new contributions."[4] Fully 600 years before Columbus, a group of Arab scholars determined that the earth is round and calculated the earth's circumference. Their conclusions were not completely accurate—they missed the true circumference of the earth at the equator by 822 miles![5]

Most Arab countries are like other countries in the Third World. The vast majority of the people are not technologically sophisticated. Yet each country has produced many scholars and scientists who are helping modernize and transform their society.

Not All Hate Americans

Three activities in the Middle East traumatized America—hostage taking, suicide bombing, and hijacking. From the hostages at the United States embassy in Iran to Terry Anderson and the other hostages in Lebanon, the abduction and detention of Americans by terrorists became a nightmare for America. Though hostages from other countries were also seized, it seemed as though the United States was the special object of hatred and anger.

In spite of Arab threats, the United States pushed to maintain a strong presence in the Middle East. In

1982 the United States joined a multinational peace-keeping force in Lebanon—and found itself in the middle of a civil war. The anger and resentment exploded on October 23, 1983, when a suicide bomber entered the marine compound at the Beirut airport and destroyed the building. The blast killed 241 marines and shattered hopes for a U.S.–sponsored settlement in Lebanon. Less than a year later the U.S. embassy near Beirut was bombed, killing fourteen people. America again seemed the favorite target for terrorist bombs.

The third strike against America came in 1985. In June, Shiite terrorists hijacked a TWA jet en route from Athens to Rome. They killed one American and held thirty-nine others hostage for sixteen days. Four months later terrorists seized the Italian cruise ship *Achille Lauro*. They killed one American passenger and terrorized the others before surrendering to Egyptian authorities. Were Americans safe anywhere in the Middle East?

The rash of hostage-taking, bombing, and hijacking made many Americans nervous. Did everyone in the Middle East hate Americans? Televised accounts gave that impression. Yet these incidents did not paint an accurate picture. Many groups in the Middle East did resent America's support for Israel and the values for which America stood. But for most individuals in the Middle East, anger at America did not translate into hatred of Americans.

The Gulf War exposed the mixed feelings toward Americans. Angry crowds burned American flags in Jordan and Iraq, while Saudis, Syrians, and Egyptians claimed America as an ally. Kuwaitis lined the streets to cheer as convoys of American soldiers rolled into Kuwait City. America found new friends in the Middle East during the Gulf War.

Arabs in the End Times

Will the Arabs ever unite? How does Arab unity relate to Bible prophecy? We will examine some countries in more detail in the next chapters, but some basic observations can be made here. First, the Bible does not picture a single Arab "nation" in the end times. Islam will not unite under a single flag. The Muslim people will continue to pay lip service to the ideal of Islamic unity, but such unity will not happen.

The prophet Daniel lifts God's prophetic veil to describe the future of the Egyptians and Jordanians. In Daniel 11 the prophet traces Gentile kings and nations that would impact his people through history. Though everything described by Daniel was still future when he wrote, much has now been fulfilled. But beginning in verse 36 Daniel portrays events that are still future.

Daniel describes the coming prince of evil who "will exalt and magnify himself above every god and will say unheard-of things against the God of gods" (Daniel 11:36). Daniel focuses especially on the final three-and-a-half-year period when this wicked ruler will try to conquer the earth and crush the nation of Israel. In verse 41 Daniel describes this king's invasion of Israel, which Daniel calls "the Beautiful Land."

The end-time evil ruler will "invade many countries and sweep through them like a flood" (11:40). But Daniel predicts that not every country will feel the fury of this terrible tyrant: "Many countries will fall, but Edom, Moab and the leaders of Ammon will be delivered from his hand" (11:41). The three countries, listed in order from south to north, sat just to the east of the Rift Valley, Dead Sea, and Jordan Valley. Today we know this land as Jordan. Jordan's capital, Amman, preserves the name Ammon.

Jordan will escape the vicious attacks of this wicked ruler. Daniel does not say why Jordan will be spared, but its people continue in relative safety during this time of terror. Some prophetic passages picture the Jews fleeing to the rugged mountains to escape the attacks of this ruler. Perhaps some will flee to the mountains of Jordan.

Jordan will escape, but Egypt will not fare as well. After noting that the wicked ruler will gain control of many countries, Daniel includes a somber warning: "Egypt will not escape. He will gain control of the treasures of gold and silver and all the riches of Egypt" (11:42-43). This final world ruler will invade and plunder Egypt and the surrounding nations. His invasion must come near the end of the three-and-a-half-year period because "reports from the east and the north will alarm him" (11:44) and force him to leave Egypt. Daniel records that, after leaving Egypt and attacking his new adversaries, this ruler will go to Israel where he "will come to his end" (11:45).

Daniel's chronology has the prince of evil leaving Egypt because of "reports from the east and the north." Daniel does not name the subject of these reports, but one possibility is rebuilt Babylon. Rebuilt Babylon will rise to power in the final seven-year period and will exert control over this wicked ruler. The Apostle John pictures this control by describing a prostitute (the city of Babylon) riding on a beast (the end-time ruler). The Bible does not record how Babylon will exert control over the world ruler, but one distinct possibility is through the control of Middle-East oil. If one individual could control the oil resources of Iraq, Kuwait, and Saudi Arabia, he would exert tremendous political pressure on the West. One could almost say he would be able to "ride the West into the ground" by controlling the flow of oil.

The wicked ruler's attack on Egypt and the surrounding Muslim countries triggers a political response from the ruler of Babylon. Perhaps the ruler of Babylon initiates an oil embargo similar to the one imposed by OPEC in 1973. Whatever the specific response, it so alarms the prince of evil that he withdraws from Egypt and moves his army to this new place of trouble. Daniel records that "he will set out in a great rage to destroy and annihilate many" (11:44).

The Apostle John picks up the story once this ruler arrives near Babylon: "The beast and the ten horns you saw will hate the prostitute. They will bring her to ruin and leave her naked; they will eat her flesh and burn her with fire" (Revelation 17:16). Babylon will be destroyed. John agrees with Daniel in placing this destruction at the very end of the seven-year period of trouble. John, like Daniel, then predicts that the evil ruler will return to Israel, where he will be destroyed as Jesus Christ returns to earth.

In spite of all efforts, the Middle East will remain a place of ferment and turmoil. Jordan will continue to vacillate between East and West, and her vacillation will allow her to remain on the sidelines. Egypt will lose her independence as the ruler from the West senses her strategic position and inherent wealth. Evidently some semblance of Muslim unity will remain intact because the nations of the "east and the north" will respond to the fall of Egypt. Possibly this will involve Babylon and the surrounding oil-producing countries. Their reaction will frighten the end-time ruler and force him to send his army against this latest threat. After crushing this final Arab uprising, he will descend on Israel to finish off the Jews. Only then will the Messiah return to earth.

C H A P T E R   T E N
SADDAM HUSSEIN AND THE RISE OF BABYLON

For eight months the world's eyes were riveted on
events in the Persian Gulf. Millions came home from
work and settled in front of their televisions to watch
the first prime-time war. The technical sophistication
of billion-dollar weapon systems created the illusion
that the war was merely a high-priced video game.
We were mesmerized for a short while, but like everything else in our society, the war could hold our interest for only so long.

Then the guns went silent, the war "officially"
ended, and the world shifted its gaze to other countries
and conflicts. Events from Barcelona to Bosnia
pushed Baghdad off the front page of the newspaper.
The New World Order holds sway as peace plans are
proposed for the Middle East.

But as the world catches its collective breath, many
are pausing to take a closer look at the events in the
Persian Gulf and trying to fit them into the larger puzzle of God's plan for this present world. What did the
war accomplish? At this time, Saddam Hussein still
controls Iraq. He has remained in power longer than

George Bush, the driving force behind the Allied coalition. Whether or not Saddam Hussein can continue to remain in power is still unclear. However, the predictions of his early and certain end were too optimistic. Indeed, he seems to be trying to undergo a political metamorphosis. Saddam Hussein the evil antagonist has gone into his cocoon and is trying to emerge as Saddam Hussein the reformed. The Butcher of Baghdad wants to make peace with the Kurds; the invader of Kuwait is now seeking closer ties with his Arab brothers; the self-styled Nebuchadnezzar is now discussing democracy for his people.

Shortly after the Gulf War, the *Los Angeles Times* polled eight Middle East experts and asked them to predict Saddam Hussein's chances of surviving politically. Most felt that Saddam Hussein could not survive for very long, but Rami Khouri, a Palestinian political columnist and author, offered unique insight into Hussein's political survivability:

> Although Hussein's military astuteness is poor, his political survival is probable. . . . He articulated and personified a new Arab-Islamic spirit of defiance and fearlessness in the face of clear enemy superiority. That spirit rested on overwhelming Arab dissatisfaction with the artificial, unnatural and failed regional economic-political order following World War I; the double standard of the United Nations and the world in applying Security Council resolutions; the legacy of the Western colonial and neo-colonial powers sending large armies to the Middle East to main-

tain an order that suits their commercial and strategic needs but does not suit the aspirations of the indigenous Arab-Muslim people; and the U.S. insistence that Israel should remain stronger than all Arab neighbors.[1]

In the early flush of victory, most of the world failed to notice that little had changed in the Middle East. No countries changed leaders. Saudi Arabia and Kuwait are still ruled by royal families who have no strong desire to establish democracies. Syria and Iraq are still ruled by Ba'ath party dictators with ambitions of extending their national borders—when the time is right. The West remains heavily dependent on oil— and over half the world's supply still rests under the sands of the Middle East. A relative calm has again returned to this region of the world. But is it the beginning of a lasting peace or only the temporary calm before the next storm?

Prophets and Soothsayers

The Persian Gulf crisis saw a renewed interest in Bible prophecy unparalleled since the 1970s. Books on prophecy made the *New York Times* best-seller list and rocketed to the top of the Christian best-seller lists. Most of the books examined events in the Middle East in light of Bible prophecy. My book *The Rise of Babylon* was one of those whose sales surpassed everyone's expectations.

But as a good friend of mine often says, "Light attracts bugs." While many books tried to examine current events in light of Bible prophecy, others tried to read Bible prophecy into current events. This distinction is subtle, but it is extremely important. As a firm believer in Bible prophecy, I am convinced that God does have a plan for this world that includes both Babylon and the nation of Israel. I also believe that, as the time for the fulfillment of those prophecies draws near, events in the world will more closely parallel events described in the Bible. However, the starting place for any comparison must be the Bible, not current events.

As the war in the Persian Gulf unfolded, many of the more spectacular "predictions" of some Bible students proved to be wrong. Operation Desert Storm was not Armageddon; Saddam Hussein was not the Antichrist, and Jesus did not return to earth to climax the battle. Those who saw Scud missiles and laser-guided bombs in the Bible found, in the end, that the battle fought in the Persian Gulf did not fulfill the end-time battle described in Isaiah 13 and Jeremiah 50–51. Was the Bible wrong? No. The problem was that these individuals misunderstood God's Word. They read current events into the Scriptures instead of using the Scriptures to evaluate current events.

Operation Desert Storm is over, but nagging doubts remain. The battle was not Armageddon, but the parallels between recent events in the Middle East and Bible prophecy were too great to ignore. Were these parallels a mere fluke of history, or are the events of the world hastening toward a predetermined conclusion? God's Word says much about Babylon and its role in the final act on the stage of history. Anyone who wants to know what will happen in the world needs to study both current events and Bible prophecy because the two are drawing closer together.

Will the Biblical Babylon Please Stand Up?

From Genesis to Revelation, Babylon occupies a prominent place in the Bible. Babylon epitomizes humanity's pride and rebellion against God. The name comes from the description of the tower around which the city was first built—*bab* (gate), *el* (god). Babel was humanity's self-appointed gateway to God, the place where they hoped to reach God by their efforts apart from His intended plan.

Babylon retained its essential nature throughout the Bible. The height of Babylon's opposition to God came when the army of Babylon destroyed Jerusalem and dismantled God's kingdom on earth. They deposed the king from the line of David and dragged him off in chains. They burned the temple of Solomon and carried off the people of Judah. Daniel described Babylon as the "head of gold" in the "times of the Gentiles"—that time when Gentile powers would rule over God's people.

But the God who predicted the triumph of Babylon also promised its ultimate destruction. The prophet Isaiah announced that "Babylon, the jewel of kingdoms, the glory of the Babylonians' pride, will be overthrown by God like Sodom and Gomorrah" (Isaiah 13:19). The city that flew so high will be brought crashing down. Babylon's fall will coincide with Israel's restoration. "The LORD will have compassion on Jacob; once again he will choose Israel and will settle them in their own land" (14:1). Isaiah's predictions have never been fulfilled.

More than a century after Isaiah cried against Babylon, the prophet Jeremiah predicted the same destruction: "'As God overthrew Sodom and Gomorrah along with their neighboring towns,' declares the LORD, 'so no one will live there; no man will dwell in it'" (Jeremiah 50:40). Jeremiah also promised that God's restoration of His people would result after Babylon's fall: "'In those days, at that time,' declares the LORD, 'the people of Israel and the people of Judah together will go in tears to seek the LORD their God. They will ask the way to Zion and turn their faces toward it. They will come and bind themselves to the LORD in an everlasting covenant that will not be forgotten'" (50:4-5).

Some scholars believe that Babylon's fall to Cyrus and the Medo-Persians fulfilled the prophecies of Isaiah and Jeremiah. But much of what these prophets predict did not happen at that time. The city did not fall suddenly, and the houses were not burned. No great slaughter of inhabitants took place. If we take the descriptions of Isaiah and Jeremiah at face value, then Cyrus's capture of the city did not fulfill their predictions. But if these declarations of doom have not yet been fulfilled, when will Babylon be destroyed?

The Babylon of Revelation

In the book of Revelation, the Apostle John weaves together the unfulfilled strands of Bible prophecy. For more than two chapters the apostle places Babylon on the loom of God's Word and pulls together the threads of Babylon's role in history and prophecy. Revelation 17–18 pictures the end of Babylon's time in the tapestry of world history. But let's look carefully at the pattern woven by John.

Understanding the relationship between Revelation 17 and 18 is essential to identifying Babylon in these chapters. Do Revelation 17 and 18 separately describe two different Babylons, as many have long held? These individuals believe that Revelation 17 describes a religious Babylon while Revelation 18 describes an economic Babylon—the capital of the end-time world leader. Or, do these two chapters speak of only one Babylon—the literal city to be rebuilt in Iraq?

The Apostle John describes the Babylon of both chapters in such a similar way that he must have only one Babylon in mind. For example:

Babylon

The name is the same.
"Babylon the Great" (17:5)
"Babylon the Great" (18:2)

The identity is the same.
"The woman . . . is the great city." (17:18)
"Woe! Woe, O great city!" (18:10)

The clothing is the same.
"The woman was dressed in purple and scarlet, and was glittering with gold, precious stones and pearls." (17:4)
"Woe! Woe, O great city, dressed in fine linen, purple and scarlet, and glittering with gold, precious stones and pearls!" (18:16)

Both hold a cup.
> "She held a golden cup in her hand, filled with abominable things and the filth of her adulteries." (17:4)
> "Mix her a double portion from her own cup." (18:6)

The relationship to kings is the same.
> "With her the kings of the earth committed adultery." (17:2)
> "The kings of the earth committed adultery with her." (18:3)

The relationship to the nations is the same.
> "The inhabitants of the earth were intoxicated with the wine of her adulteries." (17:2)
> "For all the nations have drunk the maddening wine of her adulteries." (18:3)

The relationship to believers is the same.
> "I saw that the woman was drunk with the blood of the saints, the blood of those who bore testimony to Jesus." (17:6)
> "In her was found the blood of prophets and of the saints, and of all who have been killed on the earth." (18:24)

The means of destruction is the same.
> "They will bring her to ruin . . . and burn her with fire." (17:16)
> "She will be consumed by fire." (18:8)

The source of the destruction is the same.
> "For God has put it into their hearts to accomplish his purpose." (17:17)
> "God has remembered her crimes. . . . For mighty is the Lord God who judges her." (18:5, 8)

The list of similarities between the Babylon of both chapters is impressive. Each chapter refers to a city named Babylon. Each chapter describes Babylon as a city clothed in wealth proudly flaunting her wicked heritage. Each chapter graphically pictures the illicit dealings this city will have with other nations until she receives God's final judgment. John's descriptions are of one city, not two. John has only one Babylon in mind, and it's the same city that has reared its prideful head throughout the ages.

John positions Revelation 17 and 18 in a larger context that emphasizes the unity of the chapters. John inserted chapters 17 and 18 to explain in detail the destruction of "Babylon the Great," announced by God in Revelation 16:19: "God remembered Babylon the Great and gave her the cup filled with the wine of the fury of his wrath." Revelation 17 and 18 explain this one event.

John summarizes heaven's response to Babylon's fall in Revelation 19:1-3. In this heavenly "Hallelujah Chorus," the multitude in heaven praise God because "He has condemned the great prostitute" (19:2). John described Babylon as a prostitute in chapter 17. The multitude continue to praise God as they shout, "Hallelujah! The smoke from her goes up for ever and ever" (19:3). The "smoke" that "goes up forever" pictures the burning of Babylon described in chapter 18.

Chapters 16 and 19 serve as bookends to introduce and summarize the fall of Babylon. John has only one Babylon in mind in this section, and he describes that city in great detail in chapters 17–18. Babylon will rise—and fall—again.

Babylon the Prostitute

John began his message against Babylon in Revelation 17 by painting a picture of a prostitute astride a scarlet beast. He could have entitled his masterpiece "Beauty on the Beast." John sketched his verbal portrait in the first six verses. God then sent an angel to interpret the vision in the next twelve verses. God's purpose in Revelation 17 is to explain to the Apostle John the reason for Babylon's destruction. Chapter 18 then focuses on the response to Babylon's destruction. Within these two chapters God provides four interpretive keys that help us identify Babylon.

God's first interpretive key is His description of Babylon in 17:1 as "the great prostitute, who sits on many waters." The description of Babylon as a prostitute has caused many to identify Babylon as a false religious system. But God did not identify Babylon as a prostitute to point to her religious nature. Rather, God called her a harlot to emphasize her prostitution of values for economic gain.

This evil woman of Revelation 17 sounds much like the woman of wickedness in Zechariah 5. Zechariah peered into a basket to gaze on a woman whom God identified as "wickedness" (Zechariah 5:7-8). She embodied all that was evil. Angels carried the basket "to the country of Babylonia to build a house for it. When it is ready, the basket will be set there in its place" (5:11). Wickedness, personified as an evil woman, will someday dwell again in the land of Babylon. Could John's prostitute of Revelation 17 be the fulfillment of Zechariah's prophecy?

It's a Mystery to Me

God's second interpretive key is the name written on the harlot's forehead. God calls the woman "Babylon the Great," but He also includes other descriptions in His title. He pictures Babylon as a "mystery." He also calls her the "Mother of Prostitutes and of the Abominations of the Earth" (Revelation 17:5). What do these titles mean?

Two problems must be resolved. First, in what way is this woman a "mystery"? John could either be saying that the name on the woman's forehead is "Mystery Babylon the Great." Or he could be saying that the name, "Babylon the Great," written on the woman's forehead, is a mystery. The second option fits best in the context. Whenever John names the woman elsewhere in the book he simply calls her "Babylon the Great" not "Mystery Babylon the Great" (see 16:19; 18:2).

The second problem that must be resolved is the exact nature of the mystery. In what way is "Babylon the Great" a mystery? Some feel by using the word *mystery,* God intended Babylon to be interpreted symbolically or figuratively.[2] However, in the New Testament the word *mystery* does not denote the quality or character of the truth; it focuses on the availability of that truth.

When God calls Babylon a mystery, it does not mean that Babylon is a spiritual or mystical system of evil as opposed to a literal "brick and mortar" city. God called Babylon a mystery to show that He had not revealed this truth about Babylon earlier. After describing the mystery of Babylon riding on the beast,

God's interpreting angel said to John, "Why are you astonished? I will explain to you the mystery of the woman and of the beast she rides" (17:7).

The mystery revealed to John was that two world powers (the prostitute and the beast on which she was riding) would coexist in the end times. Daniel predicted the rise of a fourth world empire (the beast) that would rule the world just before the establishment of Jesus' kingdom (Daniel 2:40-45; 7:23-27; 9:26-27). But other Old Testament prophets predicted the restoration of Babylon as a major power in God's future prophetic program (Isaiah 13–14; Jeremiah 50–51; Zechariah 5:5-11). But how could both empires exist simultaneously and fit into God's program for the world? That was the "mystery" revealed to John.

And the Woman Is . . .

God's third interpretive key is perhaps most important because it represents God's identification of Babylon. Many have offered their interpretation of the prostitute called Babylon. But any identification must begin with God's interpretation of the prostitute in Revelation 17:18. There the angel gave God's explanation of the harlot: "The woman you saw is the great city that rules over the kings of the earth." God's interpretation of the prostitute is significant because He identifies the Babylon of chapter 17 as a city, not some ecclesiastical or mystical system. Babylon must be a city of worldwide importance, for God announces that it "rules over the kings of the earth." Whatever else might be included in this end-time Babylon, God identifies it first as a city.

What about the Seven Hills?

In his portrait of "Beauty on the Beast," John writes that the beast on which the woman is sitting has seven heads. When the angel interpreted this to John he said, "This calls for a mind with wisdom. The seven heads are seven hills [mountains] on which the woman sits. They are also seven kings. Five have fallen, one is, the other has not yet come; but when he does come, he must remain for a little while" (Revelation 17:9-10).

What are the seven hills on which the woman is sitting? Traditionally many have said that the seven hills refer to the city of Rome, known in John's day as the seven-hilled city.[3] Since the woman sits on seven hills, she must be the city of Rome, not the literal city of Babylon. Is this God's interpretation?

Identifying the prostitute as Rome because of the seven hills has some serious flaws. The first flaw is the assumed relationship between the woman and the hills. The seven heads are attached to the beast, not the woman. John makes a distinction between the woman and the beast; and the seven hills are part of the beast. The angel said, "I will explain to you the mystery of the woman and of the beast she rides, which has the seven heads" (17:7). If the seven hills refer to Rome, then the most John is saying is that the world leader's end-time empire will be centered in the city of Rome. The seven hills do not identify the location of the prostitute because she is not part of the beast.

Still, some might argue that the harlot should be associated with Rome because John says the hills are "seven hills on which the woman sits." But the prostitute's sitting on the seven hills is a reference to her control, not to her location. In Revelation 17:1 the woman sits on "many waters." The angel interprets the waters in 17:15 as "peoples, multitudes, nations and languages." Her sitting on the waters is a reference to her control over all nations of the world. John also pictures the woman "sitting on a scarlet beast" (17:3). The woman sits on the whole beast, not just on the heads. Again the reference is to her control, not to her location. If the harlot's sitting clearly suggests control twice in the chapter, is it not inconsistent to give that same figure a different meaning when it occurs for a third time? It is far more consistent to view the harlot's "sitting" as describing her control over the seven mountains instead of pointing to her physical location.

Even if the seven hills are Rome, it does not mean that the prostitute is the city of Rome. In fact, there is evidence to believe that the seven hills refer to something other than the city of Rome. The symbolic nature of mountains comes from the Apostle John's Jewish heritage. John was a Jew, and the book of Revelation must be interpreted with one eye on the Old Testament: "The book of Revelation is the most thoroughly Jewish in its language and imagery of any New Testament book. This book speaks not the language of Paul, but of the Old Testament prophets Isaiah, Ezekiel, and Daniel."[4]

In the Old Testament, a mountain was often a symbolic reference to a kingdom or national power. The prophet Isaiah wrote of a time when "the mountain of the LORD's temple will be established as chief among

the mountains; it will be raised above the hills, and all
nations will stream to it" (Isaiah 2:2). In Jeremiah
51:25, God issued a stern warning to the nation of
Babylon: "'I am against you, O destroying mountain,
you who destroy the whole earth,' declares the LORD.
'I will stretch out my hand against you, roll you off
the cliffs, and make you a burned-out mountain.'"

The prophet Daniel saw a vision in which "the rock
that struck the statue became a huge mountain and
filled the whole earth" (Daniel 2:35). What did the
mountain symbolize? "In the time of those kings, the
God of heaven will set up a kingdom that will never
be destroyed, nor will it be left to another people. It
will crush all those kingdoms and bring them to an
end, but it will itself endure forever" (2:44).

The Old Testament uses the figure of a mountain to
refer to a kingdom. But there is yet another reason for
identifying the seven mountains in Revelation 17 as
seven kingdoms. The identification of the seven mountains as kingdoms best explains the dual identification
of the seven heads as both mountains and kings.

If the seven mountains refer to Rome, there is difficulty in identifying the seven kings of the vision. Who
are the seven kings of Rome? Many try to identify the
kings with the seven emperors of the Roman Empire
from Augustus Caesar to Titus. But to make the seven
mountains fit these emperors, three other Roman
emperors who reigned between Nero and Vespasian
must be omitted. This is not sound interpretation:
"Such a procedure is arbitrary, for Galba, Otho and
Vitellius, unimportant as they may have been, were
bona fide emperors and were recognized as such by

ancient historians."[5] The seven kings in John's vision do not match Rome's history.

When the angel interprets God's vision, he explains to John that each head represents both a mountain and a king. This makes sense only if the "mountain" is an expression that refers to a kingdom. The heads are seven kingdoms and the kings who rule them. We also associate a leader with his government when we talk about the "Clinton administration" or "Yeltsin's Russia."

The prophet Daniel clearly illustrates this dual identification of a kingdom with its king. In Daniel 2 the prophet interpreted King Nebuchadnezzar's dream of a multi-metaled statue: "You [King Nebuchadnezzar] are that head of gold. After you, another kingdom will rise, inferior to yours" (2:38-39). Daniel wrote that the head of gold was a king, but the second part of the statue referred to another kingdom. Daniel obviously viewed the kingdom of Babylon as personified in the king that stood before him. Thus, he could switch from the king to the kingdom with no inconsistency. The Apostle John viewed the seven kingdoms and the seven kings in the same way. The seven heads that the angel identifies as "hills" and "kings" in Revelation 17:9-10 probably refer to seven empires and their kings, not the city of Rome.

What's on the Horizon?

In Revelation 17–18, God provides vital information on an end-time power named Babylon. Babylon is first a literal city that will dominate the world. It will be characterized as a harlot that prostitutes her moral values for material luxury. God calls Babylon a mystery because He had not before revealed her relationship to the end-time ruler. Evidently she will exert control over much of the earth.

God's four interpretive keys in Revelation 17 do not unlock some mystical system of religion that will infiltrate the world. Rather, they open the door of prophecy on a brick-and-mortar city intoxicated with power and luxury. The Babylon in these chapters will rise geographically and politically.

John describes a prostitute named "Babylon the Great, the Mother of Prostitutes and of the Abominations of the Earth." God interprets this prostitute in Revelation 17:18: "The woman you saw is the great city that rules over the kings of the earth." John's Babylon is a city—a literal place located in southern Iraq that will exist in the end times.

But, with apologies to Saddam Hussein, why describe Babylon as the "mother of all prostitutes"? God's title graphically summarizes the sordid history of Babylon. Looking back to the Tower of Babel, God sees Babylon as the birthplace for all rebellion following the Flood. This city of wickedness spawned all the rebellion and false attempts to reach heaven apart from God.

John makes the dramatic prediction that Babylon will again exercise control over the world in the last days. Her control is economic. He describes Babylon as a city of incredible wealth where "the merchants of the earth grew rich from her excessive luxuries" (18:3). Babylon will exercise control over the end-time world ruler (called "the beast") and engage in illicit enterprises with "the kings of the earth" (18:9). Babylon will claw its way to the heights of power and influence one last time.

But how can the literal city of Babylon ever fulfill these predictions? After all, isn't Babylon in Iraq, and wasn't the power and prestige of Iraq destroyed for good during Operation Desert Storm? If you take the Bible at face value, you must conclude that Babylon will achieve a place of international importance in spite of Operation Desert Storm. But how can this be?

First, the city of Babylon was not destroyed or bombed during the Gulf War. The rebuilding program begun by Saddam Hussein remains intact. In fact, since the end of the war, work on Babylon has resumed. In September 1992 Iraq sent out invitations for the fourth Babylon Festival. Guests from around the world were again invited to gaze on the city Saddam Hussein continues to rebuild.

> Work is underway on a series of three huge viewing platforms just outside the walls of Nebuchadnezzar's Babylon from which visitors will be able to look down at new excavations Iraq is planning. "This is the personal orders of the President," said Iraq's Director General of Antiquities, Mouyad Said.[6]

The Bible's prophecies will be fulfilled when someone announces that Babylon will become their capital. The city does not need to be completely rebuilt. (No city is ever completely built!) The Bible says that Babylon will be in existence, will be the capital of a

Middle Eastern empire, and will be the location of incredible wealth and commerce.

Saddam Hussein has not announced that Babylon will be his capital. But whether it will be Saddam Hussein or some future ruler who will make this announcement, Babylon will again become the capital of an empire in the Middle East.

Second, Iraq is still a major military force in the Middle East. "Iraq may have been weak in comparison with the U.S. Army after its six-month buildup in the Sands of Saudi Arabia—but compared to its immediate neighbors, the Iraqi Army can still field overwhelming force."[7] Should the United States be unable or unwilling to defend the Gulf states in the future, Iraq still has the military muscle to retake Kuwait and threaten Saudi Arabia. No other world power has the ability to project enough military might into the Middle East to stop Saddam Hussein or any future successor to Hussein. Should Iraq gain control over half the world's proven oil reserves, its leader would have both the cash and the influence over the West to force the elimination of UN sanctions. The world would make peace to keep the supply of oil flowing.

Before August 1990 the world ignored the potential threat posed by Iraq. In a matter of weeks Saddam Hussein showed the world how vulnerable it really was. After the war was over most of the world assumed that the threat was gone. It's not. In January 1993 Hussein again challenged the Western coalition. As a senior Iraqi official told *Newsweek* magazine, "We accepted a cease-fire, but we never signed a surrender document with anybody. . . . What we accepted at the end of the fighting we refused to accept a year later. What we accepted a year later we do not accept now, and what we are accepting now we will refuse a year from now."[8] The Bible pictures Babylon as a major economic power in the end times, and the potential for Iraq's rapid rise is still great.

CHAPTER ELEVEN
TURKEY, IRAN, AND THE ISLAMIC ALLIANCE AGAINST ISRAEL

As the turbulent decade of the 1970s stumbled to an end, religious fundamentalism rocked the United States. But this upheaval came not from a revival among Christians in America but from militant Muslims in Iran. Ayatollah Ruhollah Khomeini, the stern-faced spiritual leader of Iran's Shiite fundamentalists, returned to his country after fifteen years in exile. Having forced the Shah of Iran off his throne, Khomeini set about to transform Iran into an Islamic republic.

The United States became the enemy of Islam and the Iranian people. On November 4, 1979, a mob stormed the U.S. embassy and seized the staff. For 443 days Americans watched helplessly as Iranian fanatics marched in the streets shouting, "Death to America," burned American flags, and imprisoned American citizens. The trauma provoked anti-Iranian sentiment in the United States that still affects American policy in the Middle East.

Saddam, Saddam, He's Our Man
The roots of the 1991 Gulf War extend back to 1979. Just five months after Khomeini returned to Iran,

Saddam Hussein assumed supreme authority in Iraq. One man was a cleric and the other was a secular revolutionary, but both shared a deep-seated sense of mission and destiny. Each man sought to change the face of the Middle East. On September 22, 1980, while America's hostages still languished in Iran, Saddam Hussein's tanks rolled over Iranian positions on the border. His invasion of Iran started the eight-year Iran/Iraq War.

Saddam Hussein received much of his military support and training from the Soviet Union while the United States had earlier equipped Iran's army with American-made weapons. But Khomeini's rise to power changed America's relationship with Iran. Though the United States remained officially neutral in the Iran/Iraq conflict, we froze Iranian assets after the mob seized our hostages. We also refused to ship any military equipment or replacement parts to Iran. Our dislike of Khomeini and Iran shaped our foreign policy.

After a string of early successes, Hussein's army sputtered and stalled. Iran's soldiers gained the offensive and pushed Iraq from much of the captured territory. By the mid-1980s, the tide had definitely turned in favor of Iran. Iraq's collapse became a distinct possibility. But the United States and other Western nations diverted disaster by coming to Saddam Hussein's aid. Several countries joined to provide Iraq with sophisticated military hardware and valuable technical data.

Why did these countries support Iraq and Saddam Hussein? They were not ignorant of his record of terrorism and human-rights abuses. Within days of assuming power, Saddam Hussein arrested and executed twenty-one of his political rivals. His rule of terror continued against the Kurdish people: "The American–West European tilt towards Iraq was maintained all the time that the Baath were busy killing their own Kurdish population."[1] Did no one see the ruthlessness and danger of Saddam Hussein?

If the rest of the world chose to ignore Saddam Hussein, Israel did not. Convinced of his evil intentions, Israel risked international condemnation to bomb the Osirak nuclear reactor near Baghdad in June 1981. Israel also funneled military hardware and supplies to the Iranians—something Khomeini and his Islamic fundamentalists never publicly acknowledged. The Israelis recognized the danger posed by Saddam Hussein's military ambitions, and they wanted to keep him contained.

Hindsight provides marvelous perspective. The Gulf War allows us to trace the rise of Saddam Hussein with remarkable clarity. But could Saddam Hussein's goals only be discerned after his invasion of Kuwait? Didn't the best intelligence services in the world see the danger in allowing Iraq to become too powerful? Why were we so obsessed with Iran that we ignored the danger of her neighbor to the west? Two reasons stand out.

First, Iran's dramatic fall to Islamic fundamentalists took the West by surprise. Khomeini's rapid rise to power and the passion of the Muslim extremists frightened and bewildered our secular society. The trauma of Vietnam overshadowed our nation, and we seemed powerless to do anything about Iran's threat to American citizens. We riveted our attention on the danger of Khomeini and Islamic fundamentalism, not on Saddam Hussein.

Second, our desire to protect our other pro-Western, oil-producing allies in the Middle East caused us to view Iran as the main threat. Khomeini's goal was to export his brand of anti-Western religious extremism throughout the Muslim world. With 50 percent of the earth's proven oil reserves ringing the shores of the Persian Gulf, his threat, if successful, had global ramifications. Would Western civilization be the next hostage taken captive by the Iranian extremists? Kuwait and Saudi Arabia seemed especially vulnerable. We had to provide a defensive shield against Khomeini—even if that shield was Saddam Hussein and the Iraqi army.

Iran: Down but Not Out

The eight-year Iran/Iraq War staggered to a conclusion in the spring of 1988. Rejuvenated Iraqi forces recaptured the Fao Peninsula in the first of three major attacks against Iranian positions. The war, and earlier religious purges, shattered Iran's economy. Inflation and unemployment rocked the country as various political factions blamed each other for their difficulties.

Khomeini himself agreed to accept a UN-sponsored cease-fire. The decision was a bitter defeat for the architect of the Islamic fundamentalist revolution. According to Khomeini, accepting the cease-fire was "more deadly than poison." But he had no choice.

Iran was but a shell of its former glory under the Shah. Nine years of Islamic fundamentalism and eight years of war had devastated the country. By some estimates Iran lost $23 billion in oil revenues because of the war. And the war forced the nation to spend an additional $24 billion on military supplies and equipment. Hundreds of thousands of Iranians died in the war with Iraq. Tens of thousands of others perished in violent political and religious crackdowns as the fundamentalists tried to "purge" Iran of *moharebeen*— the unfaithful who must be destroyed.

Iran ended the war exhausted, broke, and isolated. Her economy was devastated, her military machine was in ruins, and her prospects for recovery were bleak. The Islamic revolution was a failure. After Khomeini died, Western nations hoped that Iran had "learned her lesson" and would gradually rejoin the civilized nations of the world. Those nations are still waiting. Will Iran again become a player in the Middle East?

Since the end of the Gulf War Iran's military buildup has alarmed both her Arab neighbors and Western nations. "Iran is spending $2 billion a year to buy conventional arms, mainly from Russia and China. It is also building a nuclear, chemical, and biological weapons arsenal, and developing a long-range missile and submarine force, according to the CIA."[2] Iran's commitment to the spread of Islamic fundamentalism also continues unchecked. Her goal is to turn the entire Middle East into an anti-Western Islamic fundamentalist state. One danger in the West's attempt to destroy Saddam Hussein is that it has allowed Iran to rearm and resume her belligerent ways.

Turkey: The "Western" Islamic State

From ancient times the land of Turkey has served as the bridge between East and West. The Apostle Paul grew up in Tarsus, a city in southeastern Turkey. He later planted churches in what is today western Turkey. Paul's ministry focused on Turkey — Asia Minor — until God called him to cross the Hellespont into Europe. Today Turkey maintains that unique blend of East and West, ancient and modern, sacred and secular.

Turkey anchors the southeastern end of the NATO alliance. As such it has stood shoulder to shoulder with the West in the front line of defense against Communism. And yet the European nations have never allowed Turkey to join the Common Market or its replacement, the European Economic Community. With one foot in the West and the other in the East, Turkey tries to maintain her balance in two separate societies.

For almost 600 years the Ottoman Empire ruled the Middle East, and parts of Europe, from Istanbul. But by World War I the Ottoman Empire had become the "Sick Man of Europe." Corruption and neglect took their toll. At the beginning of the twentieth century, a reform group called the Young Turks forced the government to change. They brought many positive reforms to the Ottoman Empire, but they also led the empire into World War I on the side of Germany and Austria-Hungary.

The Allied defeat of Germany spelled the end of the Ottoman Empire. The victors gobbled up and parceled out the remains of the empire. Turkey itself went through a period of unrest until 1923, when the Republic of Turkey was finally established. Mustafa Kemal Atatürk set up the republic and made sweeping reforms. Though 98 percent of the population is Muslim, Atatürk looked to the West for his ideal of a modern nation. Turkey's new constitution did not establish Islam as the official state religion. Religious and political freedom made Turkey a Western-style democracy with close ties to Europe.

Turkey continues to look to the West for its future, but the Gulf War highlighted tensions that lie just beneath the surface. After Iraq's invasion of Kuwait, President Bush placed a telephone call to Turkey's president, Turgut Ozal. Mr. Bush wanted to apply pressure on Iraq by cutting off her oil exports. Much of Iraq's oil flows to market in a pipeline that runs through Turkey. Turkey severed Iraq's export link to the outside world, but the cost to Turkey was enormous. Turkey lost billions of dollars in revenue by closing the oil pipeline.

When he formed the Republic of Turkey, Atatürk decided to walk a fine line between East and West. One key pillar of Turkey's foreign policy was never to interfere in intra-Arab or intra-Islamic conflicts. But when President Ozal stopped the flow of Iraqi oil and allowed Allied aircraft to fly from bases in Turkey, he committed Turkey to an alliance with the West against Iraq.

Ozal's decision helped the Allied coalition in its

fight against Iraq, but the political cost was great. His popularity at home plummeted. Muslims agonized over the possibility of joining with "infidels" to fight their Islamic brothers. The drop in oil revenues from Iraq hurt the Turkish economy, and the offers of aid from Washington and other Western countries did not make up the difference. As Turkey hemorrhaged economically, the Western coalition offered a Band-Aid, and words of encouragement.

Even after the Gulf conflict ended, Turkey's problems continued to mount. After the war, more than 400,000 Kurds fled from their homeland in northern Iraq when Saddam Hussein crushed their revolt. Thousands of these refugees fled to Turkey, but Turkey had enough problems with the Kurds already living in their country. For years the Turkish government and the Kurds had fought over the Kurds' demand for an independent state of Kurdistan. Turkey's support for the Allied coalition had only compounded Turkey's conflict with the Kurds.

As the rest of the world basked in its victory over tyranny, Turkey tallied its losses. Severe economic reversals coupled with the trauma of siding against fellow Muslims tore at the nation. Ozal's pro-Western position brought his popularity to an all-time low. The nation's feeling of betrayal heightened when the expected economic aid didn't arrive but the Kurds did. Turkey had done her part to help the West, but the West had only increased Turkey's problems:

> Turkey's economic situation is worse than before the war. The impact has been greatest in lost oil

revenue, a significant drop in tourism, lost remittance from Turkish workers in the Gulf, and a shrinkage of export markets. Turkey's loss of oil revenue from shutting down the Turkish-Iraqi pipelines has been estimated at over $2 billion. Oil revenues won't return to previous levels as long as restrictions remain on Iraqi oil exports.[3]

Turkey looked to the West for help, but the West has not yet provided the necessary answers. Turkey still maintains close ties with the West, but she is now also looking in other directions for help. And that help is coming from the remnants of the old Soviet Union, Eastern Europe, and Iran.

In 1989 as East-West tensions eased, Turkey approached several Eastern European countries and republics of the Soviet Union to explore possible trade relations. With the breakup of the Soviet Union, the process accelerated. Turkey is now actively promoting the development of a Black Sea Economic Cooperation Zone. This nine-member "common market" of nations bordering the Black Sea includes Turkey, Bulgaria, Romania, and six former republics of the Soviet Union (Armenia, Azerbaijan, Georgia, Moldavia, Russia, and the Ukraine). "Blocked to the west, the Turks are looking to the north."[4]

Turkey may look north, but she also will look east. Five former Central Asian Republics of the Soviet Union have much in common with Turkey. These five republics (Kazakhstan, Kyrgyzstan, Tajikistan, Turkmenistan, and Uzbekistan) contain more than 50 million Muslims, most of whom share the same ethnic heritage and speak some variation of the Turkish language. Turkey and Iran are now vying to become the dominant influence among these recently independent Soviet republics.

Turkey's feet remain carefully planted across the Bosporus and Dardanelles. One foot rests on the Western shore with democracy, separation of church and state, membership in NATO, and a desire to join the European Economic Community. But the other foot rests in the East with common religious ties to other Muslim countries, common ethnic problems with the Kurds, and common cultural bonds with the former Central Asian Republics. Thus far Turkey has managed to keep her balance between East and West, but can she continue? Does the Bible shed any light on the future of Turkey and Iran in world history? The answer is found in the book of Ezekiel.

Islam's Attack on Israel

In chapter 7 we briefly explored Ezekiel's remarkable prophecy of an end-time invasion of Israel by a coalition of nations. It's now time to return to Ezekiel 38–39 for a closer look at the prophet's predictions. What is the prophet describing, and how does it relate to the Middle East today?

Ezekiel begins by explaining to his readers who will participate in this end-time army. In Ezekiel 38:2-3, 6, he identifies a man named Gog, who leads a coalition of nations including Magog, Meshech, Tubal, Gomer, and Beth Togarmah. Where were these countries in Ezekiel's day? The nations inhabited the rugged area north and east of the Fertile Crescent in what is today northern and eastern Turkey, northwestern Iran, and the former Soviet republics of Georgia, Armenia, and Azerbaijan. Most of the countries described by Ezekiel are today part of Turkey.

The leaders in this end-time invasion live in the area that stretches from Turkey to the land between the Black and Caspian seas. But Ezekiel also names other allies who will join these invaders: "Persia, Cush and Put will be with them" (Ezekiel 38:5). The first is "Persia." Ancient Persia is equivalent to modern-day Iran. The language spoken by Iranians today is still called Farsi, or Persian. According to Ezekiel, Iran will join this coalition of nations who will invade Israel.

The second ally identified by Ezekiel is "Cush." In Ezekiel's day the country of Cush began just south of Egypt beyond Aswan. Earlier in his ministry Ezekiel predicted that God would "make the land of Egypt a ruin and a desolate waste from Migdol [in northern Egypt] to Aswan [in southern Egypt], as far as the border of Cush" (29:10). The land of Cush stretched south from Egypt and today includes the countries we call Sudan and Ethiopia.

The final ally named by the prophet is "Put." The country of Put was located to the west of Egypt in north Africa. Ancient Put is today the country of Libya.

Many have marveled over the odd assortment of allies in Ezekiel 38–39. From Israel's perspective, the nations span the points of the compass as they unite from all sides to attack God's chosen people. The leader comes from the north, and he controls the nations concentrated around the Black and Caspian seas. Today these nations include Turkey and several republics of the former Soviet Union. This leader of the northern coalition joins forces with his allies to the east, south, and west—Iran, the Sudan, and Libya—and leads these combined forces against Israel.

For centuries the possibility of such a coalition seemed remote. Those who sought to understand the significance of Ezekiel's message tried to make sense of his prediction by looking for alternate identifications of the participants. Some searched for modern cities that matched the names given by Ezekiel (e.g., saying Meshech = Moscow). Others tried to trace the movements of nations named by Ezekiel (e.g., saying Beth Togarmah = the Germanic tribes). Their desire to understand Ezekiel's prophecy was noble, but their methods were flawed.

The best approach to interpreting God's Word is to allow the words to mean exactly what they say. Since God knew the end from the beginning, He could have named the specific countries or peoples even if they did not yet exist. For example, he told Isaiah the name of the man who would free the Jews from Babylonian captivity—Cyrus—though the man was not born until a century after Isaiah penned his name (Isaiah 45:1). The countries named by Ezekiel were well-known in his day, and God predicted that those countries would unite to attack Israel. But what could unite such a diverse group? The answer is Islam.

Exporting Islam

The collapse of the Soviet Union coincides with a

resurgence in Islamic fundamentalism. More than 50 million Muslims live in six former Soviet republics. Both Turkey and Iran are working feverishly—with Saudi Arabia—to replace Moscow as the dominant influence in these regions:

> Turkey, Iran and Saudi Arabia are the chief rivals for influence. They're vying for traditional prizes—access to markets, as well as gold, cotton and natural gas. But they're also racing to win the hearts and minds of more than 50 million Muslims newly released from 74 years of totalitarian rule. . . . How the game plays out will have profound consequences for the region—and perhaps for the world as a whole.[5]

Ezekiel's prediction takes on new relevance in light of recent events in the former Soviet Union. A northern coalition of nations united by a common religion seems entirely possible—and the two leading players are Turkey and Iran. Both nations are engaged in massive efforts to cement economic and religious ties. But they are also forging military links. A report surfaced in an Arab-language magazine that Iran used the confusion following the collapse of the Soviet Union to purchase nuclear weapons from the republic of Kazakhstan.[6] As the bonds grow closer, more religious, economic, and military links will form.

The first hints of a northern and eastern coalition are appearing on the horizon in Turkey and Iran, but what about the other allies named by Ezekiel? How do Libya and the Sudan fit in the total equation?

Recent changes in Sudan have raised concerns throughout the Muslim world. Iranian influence in Sudan is growing at an alarming rate. In the waning days of 1991 Iran's president, Hashemi Rafsanjani, led a delegation of Iranians to Sudan that included the heads of Iran's secret police and the Revolutionary Guards. Iran has already sent nearly 2,000 Revolutionary Guards to Sudan to train Sudanese army personnel. They have also shipped $17 million worth of military equipment to Sudan's army.

> Iran is trying to find some new friends in the region, and Sudan may be it.—Amir Taheri[7]

Libya's role in the Middle East remains unchanged. Muammar Qaddafi opposes Israel and will do anything to destroy the Jews. Libya has a history of harboring terrorists and helping in terrorist activities such as the 1990 bombing of Pan Am flight 007 over Lockerbie, Scotland. One can easily imagine Libya joining a group of fellow Muslims in an attack against Israel. And Libya has sent envoys to the former Soviet republics trying to establish ties with the Muslims there.

Turkey, Iran, the Muslim republics, Sudan, and Libya. Countries with little in common—except their Islamic heritage. Yet Ezekiel identifies these countries and implicates them in a plot to attack Israel. For thousands of years this alliance seemed impossible; now it is starting to form. But when will the alliance launch its attack?

D-Day

After describing who will invade Israel, Ezekiel explains when they will invade. He describes the time in general terms in Ezekiel 38:8: "After many days you will be called to arms. In future years you will invade a land that has recovered from war, whose people were gathered from many nations to the mountains of Israel, which had long been desolate." These nations will invade Israel sometime after the Jews return and resettle the land. From Ezekiel's perspective, this invasion could have occurred any time when Israel was back in the land following their return from the Babylonian captivity in 539 B.C. However, no such invasion ever took place from the time they returned in 539 B.C. until they were expelled again by the Romans. The prophecy has yet to be fulfilled.

Ezekiel adds other details to help identify when the battle will take place. Israel must be back in the land, but they also must be living in safety: "They had been brought out from the nations, and now all of them live in safety" (Ezekiel 38:8). Later God says to the invaders, "In that day, when my people Israel are living in safety, will you not take notice of it?" (38:14).

Israel will not only be living in the land and living in safety, they also will be at peace. Ezekiel describes the attackers' fiendish plan to invade unsuspecting Israel: "I will attack a peaceful and unsuspecting people—all of them living without walls and without gates and bars" (38:11). Walls, gates, and bars were protective measures taken in Old Testament times to provide security against potential enemies. Ezekiel says that the invasion will take place when Israel feels secure and unthreatened. This does not describe modern Israel. Since 1948 Israel has never felt secure enough to lower her defenses. For the past half century there has not been peace in Israel, only times when there has been an absence of war.

When will Israel ever feel at peace? The Bible describes two such periods of time still to come. The first will occur for a very short period when a coming world leader "solves" the Middle East crisis and brings peace to Israel. Described back in chapter 4, this period of relative peace will last for only three-and-a-half years. But during that time Israel will feel secure. The second time of peace will happen when Jesus Christ returns to earth to set up His kingdom of peace. During His glorious reign on earth, "He will judge between the nations and will settle disputes for many peoples. They will beat their swords into plowshares and their spears into pruning hooks. Nation will not take up sword against nation, nor will they train for war anymore" (Isaiah 2:4).

Which time of peace is Ezekiel describing? While both periods of peace end with attacks against Israel, several specific statements in Ezekiel 38–39 point to the first period of peace as the one when this invasion will occur. God allows the invasion to display His glory to Israel: "From that day forward the house of Israel will know that I am the LORD their God" (39:22). The invasion will serve as a wake-up call to the people of Israel to rouse them from their spiritual lethargy and turn them back to God. Thus the invasion must take place before their ultimate spiritual restoration. Israel is alive spiritually during the entire second period of peace when the Messiah is on earth (Isaiah 59:21; Jeremiah 31:31-34), so the battle must happen during the first time of peace while Israel is still spiritually insensitive.

Ezekiel provides a second clue when this invasion will happen. While the invasion comes when the nation of Israel is back in the land, it also takes place before all the Jews have returned to the land. After describing the battle and its aftermath, God then announces to His people, "I will now bring Jacob back from captivity and will have compassion on all the people of Israel, and I will be zealous for my holy name" (Ezekiel 39:25). One result of this invasion will be the final restoration of the Jews to the land of Israel. Since all the Jews will return to the land at the second coming of Jesus Christ to earth (Matthew 24:31), this battle must take place before the final gathering at Jesus' return.

The invasion of Ezekiel 38–39 occurs when Israel is back in the land and feeling secure. However, Israel's security is not the final time of security promised by God. Not all the Jews have returned to the land, and those who have do not really know the Lord. Only after the battle does God promise, "I will no longer hide my face from them, for I will pour out my Spirit on the house of Israel" (Ezekiel 39:29). The battle must take place in that three-and-a-half-year period when Israel will entrust her security to a world leader who has the military might to enforce world peace.

Is this day near? We simply do not know. The next event on God's prophetic timetable is the removal of

TIME LINE OF
BIBLE PROPHECY

**Church Age Ends
Believers Taken to Heaven**
1 Thessalonians 4:13-18
Revelation 3:10

Covenant with Israel Broken
Daniel 9:27b
Matthew 24:15-16
2 Thessalonians 2:3-4

**Covenant
with Israel
Confirmed**
Daniel 9:27a

**Islamic
Invasion
of Israel**
Ezekiel 38–39

Israel at Peace
Ezekiel 38:8-14

**Rise of Antichrist
& European Confederacy**
Daniel 2:40-43; 7:23-24
Revelation 6:1-2; 13:1-4

THREE-AND-A-HALF YEARS

CHURCH AGE

TRIBULATION

Christ Returns to Earth
Zechariah 14:3-5
Matthew 24:30-31
Revelation 19:11-21

Babylon Destroyed
Isaiah 13:1-22
Jeremiah 50–51
Revelation 17–18

**Final Judgment
of Humanity &
Beginning of Eternity**
Revelation 20:11–22:6

Rule of Antichrist
Daniel 7:25; 11:36-45
Revelation 13:5-8; 17:8-14

Israel Persecuted
Daniel 7:25; 9:27c
Matthew 24:17-22
Revelation 12;13-17; 13:5-7

**Christ Rules the Earth
from Jerusalem**
Isaiah 11:1-12; 65:17-25
Joel 3:17-18
Zechariah 14:8-11
Revelation 20:4-6

THREE-AND-A-HALF YEARS   ONE THOUSAND YEARS

P E R I O D   MILLENNIUM

His church from earth. In the present age, God is working on earth through His church. But God's Old Testament prophetic program centers on the nation Israel. Jesus has promised His church that He will come to take believers from this earth before these end-time events on earth begin (1 Thessalonians 4:13–5:11; Revelation 3:10). Once the church is removed, God will again resume His prophetic program for Israel.

God's prophetic clock does not begin ticking until a future world leader signs an agreement with Israel. Sometime within three-and-a-half years from the signing of that agreement the battle described by Ezekiel will occur. But world events suggest that the time is approaching. Events on the world stage parallel those pictured in the prophets. Turkey, Iran, and the Muslim republics from the former Soviet Union are forging economic, military, and religious ties. Sudan and Libya are also developing closer relationships with these countries. The world is anxious to complete a comprehensive Middle East peace plan that would guarantee Israel safety within internationally recognized borders. When world events mirror the events described in the Bible, it suggests that the beginning of the end could be near.

God versus Gog

Ezekiel not only pictures who will invade Israel and when the invasion will take place, he also describes how the invaders will be stopped. As Gog's coalition of nations descends on Israel, Israel's future hangs in the balance. Israel is caught flat-footed. Before she can even react to the threat, the invaders attack from every direction. Their well-coordinated plan takes both Israel and the world leader who vowed to protect her by surprise. How can the invasion be stopped?

God describes how the army will be stopped in Ezekiel 38:19-22. He will intervene directly to rescue Israel and destroy the invaders. Just as the attackers reach Israel, God sends a massive earthquake to this geologically fragile region: "In my zeal and fiery wrath I declare that at that time there shall be a great earthquake in the land of Israel. . . . The mountains will be overturned, the cliffs will crumble and every wall will fall to the ground" (38:19-20). With apparent victory just within their grasp, the invading armies grind to a halt as a massive earthquake causes bridges and buildings to collapse. Mountains and hillsides will slide down, blocking roads and burying those unfortunate enough to be on them at the time.

The earthquake disrupts the original plans of the invaders and causes massive communication failures. All central command and control is lost as individual units find themselves isolated and alone. The multinational mix of the armies heightens their confusion. Some invaders speak Turkish, others speak Farsi, while still others speak Arabic. In the confusion and panic the invaders mistake these other groups for the enemy and fire on their allies: "I will summon a sword against Gog on all my mountains, declares the Sovereign LORD. Every man's sword will be against his brother" (38:21). Many invaders will be killed by "friendly fire."

Two inevitable results of fighting are "plague and

bloodshed" (38:22). As the invaders fire on one
another in panic, many will be wounded and many
killed. But the earthquake will have disrupted normal
rescue and resupply efforts. The dead will remain
where they fell, and the wounded will not be evacu-
ated for treatment. Water and food supplies will run
out, and the soldiers will be forced to use whatever is
available. Conditions will be ripe for the spread of
plagues—cholera, dysentery, and all the other diseases
that come with inadequate health care and unsanitary
supplies. Many will die of their wounds or from the
diseases that follow.

God begins and ends His destruction of the invading army with "natural" disasters. The earthquake that
signaled the start of God's judgment is only the beginning: "I will pour down torrents of rain, hailstones and
burning sulfur on him and on his troops and on the
many nations with him" (38:22). God's final trio of
trouble for the invaders comes from the sky. Torrential rains will further hamper rescue efforts and kill soldiers in mudslides and flash floods. The destructive
power of water is awesome, and God will turn that
power against the invaders.

The second element of God's final disaster is hailstones. We do not think of hailstones as weapons, but
large pieces of ice hurling from the sky can do great
damage. In one Old Testament battle, God used both
swords and hailstones against Israel's enemies: "As
they fled before Israel on the road down from Beth
Horon to Azekah, the LORD hurled large hailstones
down on them from the sky, and more of them died
from the hailstones than were killed by the swords of

the Israelites" (Joshua 10:11). With no buildings still standing in which they can seek shelter, soldiers will be at the mercy of these icy missiles.

God's third danger from the sky is "burning sulfur." Ezekiel does not elaborate on this plague, but the words take us back to God's destruction of Sodom and Gomorrah: "Then the LORD rained down burning sulfur on Sodom and Gomorrah— from the LORD out of the heavens" (Genesis 19:24). The fiery destruction that devastated Sodom will again rain down on the armies invading Israel. Some feel that "burning sulfur" describes the aftermath of a volcanic eruption. This is certainly possible. Large sections of northern Israel are covered with basalt—volcanic rock that bears testimony to the "burning sulfur" that once covered the land. Large volcanic cones still dot the Golan Heights, standing as silent witnesses to the geological activity around the Jordan Valley.

Gog's invading army is no match for the mighty power of God Almighty. Israel will be spared, but the Israeli army cannot claim credit for the victory. Insurance companies describe the events that will take place as "acts of God," and the description fits. God will send an earthquake, torrential rains, hailstones, and fiery sulfur to halt this army. In panic and confusion, the soldiers will wildly shoot at one another. The devastation, coupled with a lack of medicine and supplies and poor sanitation will spawn deadly plagues. "Then they will know that I am the LORD" (Ezekiel 38:23).

Putting It All Together

God's destruction of this Islamic coalition will bring
dramatic results in the Middle East. Israel will experience a national spiritual awakening as the people realize how God protected them. The world leader had
been unable to guarantee their safety, but God was
powerful enough to intervene. Shortly after this battle
Israel will refuse to worship the statue of the world
leader that will be set up in the temple. The Bible does
not say why Israel refuses to follow her former ally,
but perhaps God uses the dramatic results of this battle
to open the eyes of His people.

Turkey, Iran, and the Islamic republics of the former Soviet Union are now fashioning their version of
a New World Order. Libya and Sudan also seek closer
ties with this group of Muslim nations. Whatever
twists and turns that relationship takes in the years
ahead, it will someday lead these countries to a disas-
trous invasion of the land of Israel.

PART THREE

EUROPE: MILITARY MIGHT AND THE NEW WORLD ORDER

The 1992 Olympic Winter Games highlighted the dramatic changes sweeping Europe. The Yugoslav team represented only part of the country that competed in the 1988 Olympics. The breakaway countries of Croatia and Slovenia each sent their own delegation of athletes. Estonia, Latvia, and Lithuania—part of the Soviet Union in 1988—competed as independent countries for the first time since the 1936 Olympics. The Soviet Union broke up so rapidly that the uniforms couldn't keep up with political events. The renamed "Unified Team" competed without flag or national anthem, but they still had the old letters "CCCP" (Russian for USSR) emblazoned on their clothes. East Germany and West Germany were no longer two separate teams. And all these earth-shattering events took place in less than four years!

Had someone predicted in the mid-1980s that Germany would reunite, the Soviet Union would peacefully break apart, and the Warsaw Pact would dissolve, he or she would have been ridiculed. Nothing seemed more permanent than the rift between Eastern Europe and Western Europe. The scars from World War II still festered as the armies faced each other across miles of barbed wire and mine fields. Yet in just a few years everything changed dramatically.

How significant are the changes in Europe? They have the potential to reorganize the balance of power and influence in the world. America and Japan seem locked in a contest for global superiority, but both may be pushed aside by the new Europe.

By the turn of the century, the European bloc will include some twenty-three nations with 520 million people and a gross domestic product of roughly $5 trillion. . . . America's GNP, in contrast, is $4 trillion, Japan's only $2 trillion; their combined population is less than 375 million.[1]

As Europe undergoes a political and economic metamorphosis, politicians and economists gaze into their crystal balls, trying to discern the outcome. Will Europe emerge as the unified giant of the new world order, or will the process produce chaos and conflict? Does the Bible provide any clues about Europe's future? In fact, the Bible does provide insight into the future of Europe and the rest of the world. Let's explore God's Word to see His explanation of Europe's destiny.

CHAPTER TWELVE
THE EEC AND EUROPEAN UNITY

A united Europe "from the Atlantic to the Ural Mountains." When Mikhail Gorbachev uttered this phrase in a Paris interview in 1989, he was echoing the words of Charles de Gaulle spoken nearly thirty years earlier.[1] For centuries scholars, statesmen, and soldiers have dreamed of a greater unified Europe. Some, such as Napoleon and Adolph Hitler, put their plans into action and plunged Europe into devastating wars. Others, such as Jacques Delors, who is president of the European Community, work quietly, almost unseen, to accomplish the same objectives without warfare. The methods differ, but the goal remains the same—a united Europe.

Can a continent with such diversity ever unite? How can countries with different languages, religious traditions, and governmental structures ever mesh into a single group? The obstacles are immense, but so are the potential rewards. The primary benefit to Europe is economic. "Perhaps the most important single cause [for unity] was the feeling that unless Europe undertook some major initiative to improve its economic and technological performance, it was doomed to fall further behind not only the United States but also, and particularly, Japan."[2]

Simply put, Europe must unite to compete in a global economy. Much like a small farmer today trying to compete with large farming enterprises, tiny countries with limited markets must unite or they will be overwhelmed by larger countries that can produce goods more economically. The countries of Europe can no longer afford to have separate product standards, separate monetary policies, or separate tariffs and import/export regulations. A central authority must have the power to establish standards and policies for all nations.

A United States of Europe?

Several attempts have been made since World War II to bring some unity to Europe. In 1948 seventeen European countries united to form the *Organization for European Economic Cooperation.* This group coordinated the distribution of aid from the Marshall Plan. But the group lacked authority to enforce its decisions. When the Marshall Plan ended, the group's effectiveness also ended.

In 1958 six nations—Belgium, France, Italy, Luxembourg, the Netherlands, and West Germany— formed the *European Community.* The goal of this community was the economic unification of Europe. They established a parliament and court of justice in Brussels, Belgium. Under this umbrella organization the countries established three separate groups. The *European Economic Community,* often called the

Common Market, worked to establish common economic policies and to drop all tariffs. The *European Coal and Steel Community* tried to coordinate the policies and practices of the coal and steel industries of the member nations. The *European Atomic Energy Community* sought to coordinate and develop atomic energy for peaceful purposes.

The organization expanded in membership, but the whole process of unification became mired in bureaucratic wrangling. By the early 1980s the lofty goals of the European Economic Community (EEC) crumbled, and the members seemed nothing more than a dispirited group of bickering nations. But the rising economic threat of the United States and Japan forced the European nations to abandon their nationalistic protectionism. They had to unite or be swept away by the technological superpowers.

In 1986 the EEC officially adopted the goal of a politically unified Europe. Considering the centuries of conflict and competition, progress has been remarkable. The countries overcame their first obstacle in 1992 when they unified product standards and eliminated tariffs and trade quotas. But these steps are only the beginning. Plans are already underway for a European central bank with a unified monetary policy for all nations. New rail and road links seek to cement the nations in this larger union, and travel restrictions between countries will be eased. From tariffs to transportation, Europe will function as a united community.

Other dramatic events that have shaken Europe in the late 1980s and early 1990s have hastened Europe's drive for unification. The collapse of the

Soviet Union and the Warsaw Pact moved Europe back from the front lines of the Cold War. The barbed-wire border that blocked the boundary between East and West has come down, and historic enemies are becoming allies.

The republics of the former Soviet Union, which once dreamed of crushing capitalism, now send emissaries to the West seeking investment capital. The hammer and sickle have fallen prey to McDonald's golden arches! Europe, freed from the fear of armed attack, can dream of a continent at peace—a dream unthinkable earlier in this century.

A Shotgun Wedding?

The architects of European unity have made remarkable progress in recent years. But not everyone is ready to write a fairy-tale ending for a United States of Europe. Many see the union to be more of a shotgun wedding than a storybook romance. Scratch beneath the surface of the hoopla and smiles, and you uncover severe problems facing European unity.

Two world wars taught most of Europe to fear the phrase *Deutschland Über Alles*—Germany over all. After World War II the victorious Allies divided and occupied Germany. Europe's bully was beaten. As the 1980s began, no one seriously believed that the two Germanys would reunite before the end of the century. But the destruction of the Berlin Wall symbolized most dramatically the collapse of the Communist empire that kept the two nations apart.

Overnight Germany became the superpower of Europe. Eighty million Germans with the largest army and the most robust economy in Europe united to overshadow the remainder of the continent. "Many of Germany's neighbors dread reunification, especially those who suffered Nazi occupation and atrocities during World War II."[3] European unity is fine in principle, but no country on the continent wants to be part of a unified Europe dominated by Germany.

The specter of Nazi Germany continues to haunt Europe, and the rise of the neo-Nazi movement among German youth troubles many outsiders. Economic stagnation and the high cost of reuniting the two Germanys has fueled the anger of young Germans. Racial violence is on the increase in Germany, and most of the violence can be traced to Nazi skinheads. Nearly 2,000 separate attacks took place in 1992 alone.[4] Can Germany be trusted to put the interests of all Europe ahead of German nationalism? "Looked to since the heady days of reunification to become 'a new superpower,' or at least the engine of growth and democratic renewal in Europe, Germany today seems too absorbed in its own identity crisis to be a leader."[5]

German unity and nationalism frighten many in Europe, but Germany is not the only country struggling with nationalism. The disintegration of the Soviet Union's empire has fanned the flames of nationalism in several parts of Europe. Croats and Serbs slaughter each other in Yugoslavia. Armenians and Azerbaijanis attack one another in the southern republics of the former Soviet Union. Basque separatists plant bombs in Spain, while members of the Irish Republican Army do the same in Britain.

Europe sprang from the soil of nationalism. Isolated tribes and confederacies united by a common language or common religious heritage form the basis of most European communities. Can these individual groups set aside their cultural and religious heritage and replace it with a larger sense of community? Or will nationalism undo any attempt to fashion a unified Europe?

The fear of a Europe dominated by Germany and the threat of rising nationalism are not the only threats to a unified Europe. Perhaps the major obstacle now is the large number of nations not included in the current organizations. The two most dominant groups seeking to shape Europe's future are the EEC and NATO. Yet only twelve European nations are members of the EEC, and only sixteen are partners in NATO. Most European countries are not members of these two organizations. But for any true European unity to succeed, it must represent all Europe.

Europe searches for the secret to a unified continent. Almost fifty years of effort have produced modest gains, but the possibility exists for remarkable progress in the remainder of this century. The rewards are enormous, but the obstacles are great. If a United States of Europe is to be formed, it will need strong leadership to forge the various nations into a political union. An umbrella organization must emerge to unify the major nations of the continent. Can such a union be fashioned?

Daniel's "Times of the Gentiles"

The prophet Daniel was God's spokesperson in the court of Babylon. Born into one of Jerusalem's leading families, Daniel was carried off to Babylon as a royal hostage in 605 B.C. He rose rapidly to become a leading statesman in Nebuchadnezzar's government. Yet we remember Daniel more for his prophecies than we do for his government service. Daniel's veiled visions of the future perplex and confuse many readers. Can we make sense of Daniel's dreams?

Daniel's prophecies make more sense when we understand the structure of his book. Daniel wrote his first chapter in Hebrew, and the chapter serves as an introduction to the book. In it we learn how Daniel came to be in Babylon and why he received God's blessing on his life. But beginning in chapter 2, Daniel changes both languages and topics. In 2:4 Daniel switches from writing in Hebrew to writing in Aramaic ("Then the astrologers answered the king in Aramaic"). The languages are similar, but the effect on Daniel's readers is as dramatic as if he had switched from writing in English to writing in French. Daniel wrote chapters 2–7 in Aramaic before switching back to Hebrew at the beginning of chapter 8.

Why the switch in language? In chapters 2–7 Daniel wrote of events important to all nations, so he wrote in the common commercial language of his day. Beginning in chapter 8, he focused on events related especially to the people of Israel, so he switched back to Hebrew. Chapters 2–7 focus on events relating to the "times of the Gentiles."

God allowed Nebuchadnezzar and the Babylonians to destroy the kingdom of Judah and carry off the Jews into captivity. God's purpose for the nation of Israel had always been the establishment of His kingdom on earth with the coming of Israel's Messiah. But because of the nation's disobedience, God punished the people by allowing them to be defeated and deported. Daniel wrote to announce to the Jews that, in spite of their circumstances, God was still in control and working out His plans for the world. God's kingdom would yet come, and the Jews would one day be restored to the land of Israel.

Daniel wrote the Aramaic section of his book to explain to the Jews (and others who might read his work) that God's kingdom was still coming. When he interpreted Nebuchadnezzar's dream in chapter 2, Daniel explained the meaning of the stone that destroyed Nebuchadnezzar's stately statue: "In the time of those kings, the God of heaven will set up a kingdom that will never be destroyed, nor will it be left to another people" (Daniel 2:44). In chapter 7 Daniel pictured "one like a son of man" coming to destroy the beasts roaming the world. "He was given authority, glory and sovereign power; all peoples, nations and men of every language worshiped him. His dominion is an everlasting dominion that will not pass away, and his kingdom is one that will never be destroyed" (7:14).

In Daniel 2–7 the prophet explains what will happen between the time when the kingdom of Judah was destroyed and God's future kingdom is finally established. This is the period commonly called the "times of the Gentiles"—a time when Gentile powers rule over the Jews and control the land of Israel and the city of Jerusalem. Daniel weaves his message together using three sets of parallel chapters to trace God's sov-

ereign plans for the "times of the Gentiles." His outline follows a typical Hebrew pattern where the first
and sixth, second and fifth, and third and fourth items
are parallel. The structure can be pictured in the following way.

Chapter 2—God's Outline of Gentile History: "The
Times of the Gentiles"
 Chapter 3—Persecution and Supernatural Protec-
tion of God's People
  Chapter 4—God Shows Gentile Rulers that
He Is Still Sovereign
  Chapter 5—God Shows Gentile Rulers that
He Is Still Sovereign
 Chapter 6—Persecution and Supernatural Protec-
tion of God's People
Chapter 7—God's Outline of Gentile History: "The
Times of the Gentiles"

The Four Nations

In the first and last chapters of Daniel 2–7 the prophet
provides insight into the Gentile powers that will rule
Israel and the Jews from the time of Nebuchadnezzar
till the coming of God's kingdom for Israel. Chapter 2
pictures the nations as four parts of a giant statue,
while chapter 7 describes the nations as four beasts
climbing from the sea. Can we interpret these visions
with any degree of certainty, or do they defy explanation?

According to Daniel, we ought to be able to interpret his visions. After describing the statue smashed
by a stone, Daniel interprets the vision: "This was the

dream, and now we will interpret it to the king" (Daniel 2:36). In chapter 7 the vision confuses Daniel until an angel comes and interprets it for him. "So he told me and gave me the interpretation of these things" (7:16).

We shrink back when we read of multi-metaled statues or beasts that seem to leap from the pages of horror novels. Somehow we imagine Daniel eating a pepperoni pizza before going to bed and recording his nightmares to frustrate the saints throughout history. Daniel's visions may be bizarre, but they are not incomprehensible. After each vision God interpreted the various parts, and His interpretation makes perfect sense when we examine it carefully.

What was the four-part statue seen by Nebuchadnezzar in his dream in Daniel 2? Daniel explained each part to the king. The head of gold represented Nebuchadnezzar himself: "You are that head of gold" (2:38). The times of the Gentiles began when Nebuchadnezzar invaded, conquered, and deported the Jews from the land of Israel. Nebuchadnezzar, as the leader of the country that destroyed Israel, took top honors in the line of Gentile nations.

Having interpreted the head of gold, Daniel moved to the second part of the vision—the chest and arms of silver. Why did the statue switch to another, less-precious metal? "After you, another kingdom will rise, inferior to yours." Nebuchadnezzar's Babylonian Empire would be replaced by another kingdom. But what kingdom replaced Babylon in history? Daniel provides the answer within his book because he lived to see Babylon fall. On October 12, 539 B.C., Babylon fell to Cyrus, king of the Medo-Persian Empire (5:30-31). Daniel described this second empire as "the kings of Media and Persia" (8:20).

After Daniel interpreted the meaning of the first two sections of the statue in chapter 2, he described the third part of the vision. The statue had "its belly and thighs of bronze" (2:32). Daniel's explanation of the belly of bronze is very brief: "Next, a third kingdom, one of bronze, will rule over the whole earth" (Daniel 2:39). In the far recesses of our minds we remember reading in world history that the Medo-Persian Empire fell to the Greek conqueror Alexander the Great. Could the Greek Empire be the third part of the statue? Daniel again confirms this sequence in chapter 8 when he names the empire that would follow Medo-Persia. Daniel identifies the empire (pictured in chapter 8 as a "shaggy goat" who would destroy the Medo-Persian Empire) as "Greece" (8:21).

Babylon, Medo-Persia, and Greece. Daniel describes the first three empires in the "times of the Gentiles." All three controlled the Middle East and ruled over the land of Israel. Daniel finally comes to the fourth part of his vision, the "legs of iron." Daniel again explains that the new metal on the statue represents a kingdom: "Finally, there will be a fourth kingdom, strong as iron" (2:40). Daniel doesn't name this fourth kingdom in his book, but the empire that defeated the Greeks, conquered the Middle East, and controlled the land of Israel was Rome. But can we know for certain that Rome is the fourth empire?

Two pieces of evidence allow us to identify Rome as the fourth empire in Daniel's vision. First, Daniel explained that when the kingdom of God—pictured as a stone—finally came "it struck the statue on its feet of iron and clay and smashed them" (2:34). This fourth empire would be the empire ruling over Israel when God's kingdom comes to earth. When Jesus came to Israel and announced, "Repent, for the kingdom of heaven is near" (Matthew 4:17), Rome was ruling over Israel.

Second, we have the testimony of the Jewish historian Josephus, who provided his interpretation of Daniel's vision. Josephus lived just after the time of Jesus and participated in Israel's ill-fated rebellion against Rome. Josephus surrendered to Rome and endeared himself to the Roman general Vespasian, who later became emperor. Josephus wrote an account of the history and wars of the Jews. Part of his project was to show Rome that Romans and Jews had much in common—in spite of their recent war. Josephus went out of his way to emphasize every event that illustrated the close historical ties between Rome and the Jews. He also tried to explain away or minimize every event that pitted the Jews against Rome.

Josephus provided a remarkable explanation of Nebuchadnezzar's statue in Daniel 2. He noted that the head of gold represented "thee [Nebuchadnezzar], and the kings of Babylon that have been before thee." While not naming Medo-Persia as the second kingdom, he clearly had this two-part nation in mind when he wrote that "the two hands and arms signify this, that your government shall be dissolved by two kings." He avoids naming Greece, but he takes care to explain that this third kingdom of bronze comes "from the west." While Josephus does not explicitly identify the fourth part of the statue as Rome, he reveals his understanding when he tries to explain away the stone that will destroy the fourth empire: "Daniel did also declare the meaning of the stone to the king; but I do not think proper to relate it, since I have only undertaken to describe things past or present, but not things that are future."[6] Rome was the "present" power, but Josephus did not want to antagonize his hosts by explaining that God's final Messianic kingdom would destroy Rome!

In Daniel 2 the prophet describes four empires that bridge the gap from the time Israel goes into captivity until the kingdom of the Messiah arrives. The four— Babylon, Medo-Persia, Greece, and Rome—form an unbroken line of descent from Daniel's day till the time of Christ.

In Daniel 7 the prophet describes the four nations as beasts emerging from the sea. The description may be different, but the same nations are in view. The first beast had the form of a lion with the wings of an eagle—two animals that symbolized the supremacy of this first kingdom. Even in ancient days the lion was celebrated as the "king of beasts," while the eagle was enthroned as the master of the air. Daniel notes that the beast ruled supreme until "its wings were torn off" (Daniel 7:4). This description pictures the humbling of Nebuchadnezzar and Babylon that the prophet records in detail in Daniel 4–5.

The prophet's second creature resembled a bear "raised up on one of its sides" (7:5). This lopsided bear pictured the two halves of the Medo-Persian

Empire, with the Persian part of the empire being the more prominent. The bear "had three ribs in its mouth between its teeth"—picturing Medo-Persia's conquest of Lydia, Babylon, and Egypt.

Daniel's third creature from the sea "looked like a leopard" (7:6). The swift leopard was an apt description of the Greek Empire that swept through the world under Alexander the Great. The leopard's "four heads" visualize the final form of Alexander's empire. His kingdom was parceled out among four generals after his death.

Daniel cannot describe the fourth creature. His animal remains unidentified except for his observations that the beast had "large iron teeth" and "ten horns" (7:7). Daniel's use of "iron" ties this fourth beast with the fourth part of the statue in chapter 2. The beast represents Rome.

The Empire Strikes Back

Daniel dramatically predicted that Rome would be the "bully on the block" when the Messiah came to earth to establish His kingdom. Just as God predicted, Rome controlled the land of Israel when Jesus came as the Jews' Messiah. But something seemed to go tragically wrong. Instead of ushering in the kingdom, Jesus was crucified. The mob, incited by the religious leaders, shouted, "Take him away! Crucify him! . . . We have no king but Caesar" (John 19:15).

Had God made a mistake? Was His kingdom program in shambles? The answer is no! Indeed, Daniel predicted that the Messiah would be killed. In Daniel 9 the prophet predicted the time sequence for God's prophetic activities. He first predicted the time "from the issuing of the decree to restore and rebuild Jerusalem until the Anointed One, the ruler" (Daniel 9:25). Daniel's prophecy pointed to the day Jesus rode into Jerusalem as Israel's Messiah.

But Daniel goes on to predict, almost 600 years before the event, what would happen to the Messiah: "After the sixty-two 'sevens,' the Anointed One will be cut off [killed] and will have nothing" (9:26). Jesus' death was no accident. God predicted the Messiah would die. But why did He die? The prophet Isaiah answered that question:

> But he was pierced for our transgressions, he was crushed for our iniquities; the punishment that brought us peace was upon him, and by his wounds we are healed. We all, like sheep, have gone astray, each of us has turned to his own way; and the LORD has laid on him the iniquity of us all. (Isaiah 53:5-6)

The Messiah died as the substitute for our evil. He went to the cross to pay the penalty for our sin.

God arranged the world's stage so that Jesus could offer Israel her kingdom at His first coming to earth. Had Israel truly repented and accepted her Messiah, God could have brought His plans to pass. But Israel rejected her Messiah, and God used this rejection to accomplish His larger plan of having the Messiah die for the sins of the world. But what does all this have to do with Rome?

For much of my ministry I taught at Dallas Theo-

logical Seminary. Each week to prepare for my
classes I organized my slides, arranged my overheads,
collated my handouts, and reviewed my notes. But
there have been times when my plans to teach have
been interrupted. Freak ice storms have blown into
Dallas the evening before my class, snarling traffic,
closing the school, and postponing my class until its
next scheduled meeting time. But when that new day
rolled around, I resumed my class where I left off.

Often, when a scheduled event does not take place,
it is rescheduled for a later time. In fact, this is what
God did with the establishment of His kingdom. Jesus
will come to earth a second time. The kingdom promised by God will be established then. And the Gentile
power controlling the land of Israel when the Messiah
comes will be the same power that was in control at
Jesus' first coming. Rome will rise again.

How do we know that a new Roman Empire will
control Israel? Three pieces of evidence lead me to
this conclusion. First, Daniel's predictions of the coming kingdom in Daniel 2 and 7 did not end at the first
coming of Jesus. The kingdom pictured by Daniel is
not the present age of the church. We are not in an age
when "the sovereignty, power and greatness of the
kingdoms under the whole heaven will be handed
over to the saints, the people of the Most High"
(7:27). The Messianic kingdom announced by Daniel
is still future, and Daniel says that when it comes,
Rome will be the country crushed by its appearance.

A second reason for seeing a renewed Roman
Empire in the last days comes from Daniel 9. As mentioned earlier, Daniel provided an amazing timetable

for Israel in this chapter. He first predicted the time
between the rebuilding of Jerusalem following her
captivity in Babylon and the revelation of her Messiah. But Daniel placed a gap between these first 483
years of Israel's prophetic history and the final seven
years of her history. Three events take place in this
gap that Daniel describes in 9:26. First, the Messiah is
to be "cut off" or killed. This happened when Jesus
was crucified. The second event in Daniel's gap is the
destruction of Jerusalem. "The people of the ruler who
will come will destroy the city and the sanctuary."
The Roman army led by Vespasian and Titus
destroyed Jerusalem in A.D. 70. Daniel then predicted
a time of trouble for the Jewish people: "War will continue until the end, and desolations have been
decreed."

After picturing this gap in God's prophetic calendar, Daniel describes the exact moment when God's
clock again begins to tick. The final seven years in
Israel's wait for her kingdom begins when "He will
confirm a covenant with many for one 'seven' "
(9:27). The final seven-year period starts when someone makes an agreement with the nation of Israel. But
who is the individual Daniel simply calls "he"? The
nearest antecedent is found in the previous verse
where Daniel spoke of "the people of the ruler who
will come" who destroyed Jerusalem and the temple.
The "he" of Daniel 9:27 is this coming ruler who
makes an agreement with Israel. The only identification Daniel provides is that this ruler's "people"
destroyed Jerusalem in A.D. 70. Since we know that
Jerusalem was destroyed by the army of the Roman

Empire, we have one sure clue for identifying the end-time ruler who will protect—and later persecute—Israel. He will come from the Roman Empire. Daniel 9:26-27 agrees exactly with Daniel 2 and 7.

Our third piece of evidence for a revived Roman Empire comes from the book of Revelation. John wrote the book of Revelation at the end of the first century A.D. God gave John an outline of what he was to write. "Write, therefore, what you have seen, what is now and what will take place later" (Revelation 1:19). John had already described his vision of the glorified Son of God, Jesus Christ, in chapter 1. In chapters 2–3 John wrote seven letters to seven churches that existed in his day. These churches shared characteristics that we find in churches throughout the past 2,000 years.

But beginning in chapter 4 the Apostle John begins a new section in his book: "And the voice I had first heard speaking to me like a trumpet said, 'Come up here, and I will show you what must take place after this'" (Revelation 4:1). Beginning here the word *church* vanishes from the book of Revelation and does not reappear until John begins to write about eternity. Instead, John begins writing about those who will be sealed from "the tribes of Israel" (7:4), "two witnesses" who will minister in Jerusalem (Revelation 11), and "a woman clothed with the sun, with the moon under her feet and a crown of twelve stars on her head" (12:1)—imagery right from Genesis 37 that pictures the nation Israel. In Revelation 4–19 John provides additional information on the final seven-year period of trouble described by the prophet Daniel.

In Revelation 13 John pictures the end-time evil empire that will control the earth. He describes the empire as "a beast coming out of the sea" (13:1). That's exactly how Daniel described the empires in Daniel 7! As John describes this end-time empire, it becomes obvious that he is describing the fourth beast of Daniel 7. John's beast has "ten horns and seven heads" (13:1), while Daniel said his fourth beast "had ten horns" (Daniel 7:7). Daniel interpreted the horns on his beast: "the ten horns are ten kings" (7:24). John provides the same interpretation for his ten horns when he interprets them in Revelation 17: "The ten horns you saw are ten kings" (17:12).

Daniel explains how long his fourth beast will persecute the people of Israel: "The saints will be handed over to him for a time, times and half a time" (Daniel 7:25). A "time" is symbolic of a year, so "a time, times and half a time" could be translated "a year, two years, and half a year." Daniel's fourth empire will persecute Israel for three-and-a-half years—the same amount of time the "ruler who will come" persecutes Israel in Daniel 9:27. As John describes his end-time evil empire, he writes that it will be allowed to "exercise his authority for forty-two months" (Revelation 13:5). Forty-two months is exactly three-and-a-half years.

Both Daniel and John describe the same empire. They picture a beast rising from the sea with ten horns representing a ten-nation confederacy. Both predict that this empire will persecute the nation of Israel for three-and-a-half years. We learned earlier that Daniel's fourth empire was Rome. Since John is describ-

ing events that are still future, he is predicting that
Rome will again be around in the end times as a major
military power. Rome will rise again.

Is the EEC in Bible Prophecy?

Is the EEC the ten-nation confederacy predicted in
Daniel and Revelation? In its present form it is not.
Twelve nations now form the EEC, and several others
have applied for membership. The Bible predicts one
diverse empire ruled by the end-time dictator. This
empire will be composed of at least ten nations who
will ally themselves with this ruler. No such align-
ment exists today.

But in the past decade Europe has changed dramatically. The iron curtain crumbled. Established countries like Yugoslavia broke apart while the two
Germanys reunited. The continent is undergoing
major political upheavals, and no one knows the outcome—no one, that is, except God.

God makes three assertions about the final European power that will play a role in end-time events.
First, the empire will be a potent military force in the
world. The rest of the world will look at the final
world ruler and his European empire and say, "Who
can make war against him?" (Revelation 13:4). At the
present time the United States is recognized as the
leading military-industrial powerhouse on the earth.
But the United States will be replaced by this
European empire.

Second, the empire will be strong militarily and economically, but it will be a fractured empire. The final
European power will still be plagued by the national-

ism that has always divided Europe. The language barriers, and long-standing political, religious, and national rivalries will make the empire difficult to govern. The Achilles' heel of this military juggernaut will be its factionalism. This is why Daniel pictured this final empire as a mixture of iron and clay. It will have the military strength of iron, but the clay represented the nationalism that would weaken the empire: "And just as you saw the iron mixed with baked clay, so the people will be a mixture and will not remain united, any more than iron mixes with clay" (Daniel 2:43).

Third, the empire will be hampered by its reliance on the Middle East. The Apostle John pictures the revived Roman Empire dominated by a Middle Eastern power centered in Babylon. In Revelation 17 John describes the Middle Eastern power (pictured as a prostitute) riding on the revived Roman Empire (pictured as a beast). In Revelation 17 Babylon sits on the beast, the heads, and many waters. John explains that her sitting on these items shows her control over them. In some sense Babylon "rules over the kings of the earth" (17:18), including this European empire.

How can Europe, in spite of its great military power, be ruled by someone from the Middle East? John cannot be saying that the ruler from Babylon physically conquers Europe, because he has already said that no one can defeat this end-time power militarily (13:4). John does not say in what way Babylon will ride over Europe, but one possibility is economic control through oil. Europe is still heavily dependent on Middle Eastern oil. If someone in the Middle East could limit the West's access to oil, he could exert strong control over this final European power.

The EEC as we see it today is not in Bible prophecy, but the goals of the EEC coincide with the Bible's predictions of an end-time power centered in Europe. A unified Europe—the economic and military powerhouse of the world—looms just over the horizon. All that is lacking is a strong personality to galvanize and unify the various factions on the continent. And that person is coming!

CHAPTER THIRTEEN
MAN OF PEACE/MAN OF POWER

The signatures on the document sealed the fate of
Czechoslovakia. Britain's prime minister, Neville
Chamberlain, signed over much of Czechoslovakia's
land and most of her industry to Adolf Hitler to
appease Hitler's demand for a greater Germany. On
his return to England, Chamberlain proudly announced that the accord he had negotiated would
bring "peace for our time." Eleven months later Hitler
broke his word and invaded Poland. World War II
began, and Chamberlain left office in disgrace. His
efforts to promote "peace at any price" plunged
Europe into war.

Why Can't We Have Peace Today?

The world longs for peace, yet we seem to follow a
vicious cycle of warfare and violence. Why can't the
world be at rest? The reasons for warfare are many,
but five major causes account for most problems
today. First, economic inequities produce conflicts between "have" and "have not" nations. Hard economic
times create international conflict even in affluent

nations. The recession of 1991–1992, coupled with
the presidential election, produced much "Japan bash-
ing" and calls for an "America first" trade policy. Similar economic problems are spawning violence in
France, Germany, Great Britain, and other countries
that are faced with rising debt and lowering standards
of living.

The second cause for national and international
strife is social, cultural, or racial intolerance. Since the
Tower of Babel, humanity has divided into separate
ethnic communities. These separate communities have
responded to those who are "different" with bigotry,
prejudice, and hatred. Even the United States today
resembles a pressure cooker more than a melting pot.
Fear and distrust among different ethnic and racial
groups is rising at an alarming rate.

The third cause for worldwide violence is religious
and spiritual hatred. The Arab/Israeli conflict could
have been solved long ago were the problem not
rooted in the religious beliefs of both groups. Jerusalem is a city sacred to both—and neither side will
agree to a peace that does not allow them to control
their holy city. The conflicts in Northern Ireland,
India, Sudan, Yugoslavia, or Armenia and Azerbaijan
are, at their core, rooted in religious differences.

A fourth cause for conflict in the world is the general decline in spiritual and moral values. The rise in
drug and alcohol abuse, the acceptance of sexual
promiscuity, and the increase in violence on television
and in the movies have one thing in common: they all
mirror a departure from traditional standards of right
and wrong. Yet the demand for absolute freedom

from any moral standards cannot free humanity from the consequences of sin. The dramatic rise in sexually transmitted diseases, AIDS, broken homes, sexual abuse, and murder is a dramatic reminder that we will be held accountable for the consequences of our actions.

The fifth cause for national and international strife is a lack of strong leadership. The Gulf War served as the dramatic exception to what otherwise has been a time of declining leadership. Leaders today may promise to provide solutions to life's problems, but all too often the leaders themselves are more intent on reading the latest poll to see which way the winds of public opinion are blowing. The world admired Mikhail Gorbachev, but the average Russian cared more about bread than *perestroika*. Gorbachev had to go. As long as the world rewards leaders for doing what is expedient and penalizes them for doing what is right, the world will be cursed with ineffective leaders.

What the World Needs Now

At the close of the Gulf War, President George Bush's plan for a New World Order seemed within the world's grasp. He envisioned a time when nations could solve their problems without warfare and bloodshed—an era when nations could work together for the common good of all. These were great and lofty ideals, but they shriveled under the harsh light of a world recession and growing cries for nationalism and protectionism. Everyone agreed in theory to an international community without barriers or battles. But Croats and Serbs, Armenians and Azerbaijanis, Irish

Protestants and Catholics, and a host of other ethnic
and religious groups could not put international good
above their need for self-preservation.

What will it take to bring peace to this planet? Are
the problems so massive that they have overwhelmed
the very systems we have put in place to provide
peace and stability? The Club of Rome, a group of
one hundred individuals from fifty-three countries
who represent a wide spectrum of cultures, ideologies,
and professions, met to discuss the problems facing
our world. Their concluding analysis of the world's
current problems sounded a note of alarm.

> Never in the course of history has humankind
> been faced with so many threats and dangers: cat-
> apulted unprepared into a world where time and
> distance have been abolished, man is sucked into
> a planetary cyclone swirling with seemingly un-
> related factors, the causes and the consequences
> of which form an inextricable maze.[1]

Can we solve the problems?

As the world sinks into the pit of moral failure,
environmental disaster, and ethnic tension, the desire
for a strong world leader will grow. History records
that many dictators rose during times of chaos and
unrest. Napoleon seized control of France following
the confusion of the failed French Revolution. The
Germans hailed Hitler as the savior of a Germany
racked by the Great Depression and humiliated by her
enemies following World War I. Lenin and Stalin
gained an iron grip on Russia by exploiting the frustra-

tions of the oppressed masses and by promising economic stability and security. Economic hardship and political turmoil breed national messiahs who galvanize their followers with promises of saving their country from ruin.

The Bible describes one such individual who plays a major role in God's end-time program for the world. He goes by several aliases, including the "ruler who will come" (Daniel 9:26-27), the "man of lawlessness" (2 Thessalonians 2:3), the "antichrist" (1 John 2:18), and the "beast" (Revelation 13:2). The Bible paints a complex portrait of this individual who will take the world by storm—and lead the final rebellion against God.

Time Magazine's Man of the Year

The distinction by *Time* magazine as Man of the Year seemed entirely fitting. If ever a leader was destined for greatness, he fit the part. He first gained public recognition when he worked to galvanize and stabilize Europe. His new Confederation of Europe, which replaced the EEC and NATO, was a political masterstroke. With the sudden economic collapse of the United States, this European confederation stepped in to assume the mantle of world leader.

Troublesome times demand strong leadership—and strong leadership was needed to impose order amid chaos. At first many countries and groups opposed his plan for economic unity. Some threatened military action to block the unification of Europe, but in the end most capitulated. However, three nations chose not to accept the inevitable, and they were crushed by the combined military might of the former NATO forces.

But *Time* did not choose him as Man of the Year merely for his success in uniting Europe. His efforts to promote peace in the Middle East and to impose a settlement on Israel and her Arab neighbors diffused a potential powder keg. Everything he did seemed to prosper—as though God Himself was pleased with him.

Certainly he deserved to be *Time* magazine's Man of the Year. On a globe cursed with petty despots and bickering politicians, here was an individual who carried himself with dignity and respect. He thought in global terms, and he made strategic decisions. All the world marveled at his power and influence. But who is this great leader?

Time magazine has not yet named him Man of the Year, but 2,000 years ago the Apostle Paul identified him as the "man of lawlessness." Today most people would call him the Antichrist. If God's end-time program is near, he could already be alive and in some position of power. His actual identity will not be revealed until he signs the seven-year treaty with the nation of Israel. But while we may not know his human identity, the Bible does share much about his character and conduct. Let's take a glimpse at God's portrait of the world's final dictator.

Winner of the Nobel Peace Prize

As a speaker and author, I am often invited to speak around the country. When I meet people who have never seen me before, I can almost predict their

response. "Oh! You're so young! Somehow I was
expecting someone much older." I do not fit the mental image they have of some grey-haired scholar. All
of us have, at times, been surprised when we met
someone who did not match the mental picture we
had formed of them. This also will be true of the
future Antichrist.

What is your image of the final world dictator?
Some picture him as Satan incarnate—a man sprout-
ing horns and a tail who is evil personified. Others see
him as a modern Adolf Hitler, a diabolical fanatic who
will brazenly crush and destroy those who oppose
him. Still others look for a foul-mouthed egomaniac, a
shameless self-promoter who will be as much con
man as conqueror. At some point in the final seven-
year period, all these characteristics will be evident.
But none of these picture the first impression the
world will have of the Antichrist.

Satan is the prince of darkness, yet Paul warned the
Corinthians that "Satan himself masquerades as an
angel of light" (2 Corinthians 11:14). The undiscern-
ing can be fooled by Satan's outward appearance.
Only after it's too late do they cry, "Oh! You're
Satan! Somehow I was expecting someone much dif-
ferent." The Antichrist will be guided and gifted by
Satan, and Satan will provide a suitable cover for his
evil emissary. What sort of first impressions will the
Antichrist make?

Daniel 9 gives the first clue by which the Antichrist
can be clearly identified. The world will not know
who the Antichrist is until "he will confirm a covenant
with many for one 'seven'" (9:27). When the world

gets its first glimpse of the Antichrist, he will be in the role of peacemaker. Obviously he will have risen to power earlier so he can make such an agreement, but this is the first time when he will be clearly identified to the world.

What is this "covenant" that the Antichrist will make with Israel? Daniel does not specify its content, but he does indicate that it will extend for seven years. During the first half of this time Israel feels at peace and secure, so the covenant must provide some guarantee for Israel's national security. Very likely the covenant will allow Israel to be at peace with her Arab neighbors. One result of the covenant is that Israel will be allowed to rebuild her temple in Jerusalem. This world ruler will succeed where Kissinger, Carter, Reagan, Bush, and other world leaders have failed. He will be known as the man of peace!

How ironic that the man who will cause so much misery and destruction appears first as a leader for world peace. He could very well be nominated for the Nobel Peace Prize for settling one of the most difficult conflicts in the world. While the world watches for a tyrant, the Antichrist appears as a trusted leader who promises peace.

Master Political Strategist

The Antichrist will arrive on the world scene with an olive branch, but concealed beneath the branch is a sword. His conquest of other nations will soon overshadow his covenant with Israel. In Daniel 11 the prophet tore off the facade to reveal the underlying motives of the Antichrist. His actions will stem from

his pride and his thirst for power. Though he might
appear initially as a man of humility, his ultimate goal
in all his actions will be to exalt himself. "He will
show no regard for the gods of his fathers or for the
one desired by women [a deity worshiped by women],
nor will he regard any god, but will exalt himself
above them all" (11:37). The Antichrist will be the
ultimate product of the "Me" generation.

His pride will only be matched by his need for absolute power. Instead of honoring any supposed gods,
"he will honor a god of fortresses; a god unknown to
his fathers he will honor with gold and silver, with precious stones and costly gifts" (11:38). The Antichrist
will spend his money on weapons of war. His strength
will come from fortresses, not from faith in God.

World events will seem to vindicate this leader's
faith in bombs and bullets. Daniel describes a series of
coalitions that rise against the Antichrist during the
seven-year period. But these other alliances are no
match for the power of the end-time ruler. "He will
invade many countries and sweep through them like a
flood. He will also invade the Beautiful Land [Dan-
iel's name for Israel!]. Many countries will fall, . . .
He will extend his power over many countries"
(11:40-42).

The Apostle John also describes the Antichrist's
reliance on military might and power. In Revelation 6
John pictures the events that inaugurate the seven-year
Tribulation period. The era begins with a rider bent on
worldwide conquest. "I looked, and there before me
was a white horse! Its rider held a bow, and he was
given a crown, and he rode out as a conqueror bent on

conquest" (Revelation 6:2). The rider is the Antichrist, and his program of worldwide domination begins at the start of the Tribulation period. He appears as a man of peace, but his desire is to dominate the world.

Satanic Counterfeit

Our analysis of the Antichrist would not be complete without another observation. He may come appearing to be a man of peace, and he may be motivated by pride and a thirst for power. But any success he achieves is due largely to supernatural forces at work behind the scenes. Ultimately he is a pawn in the hand of Satan.

The Apostle Paul provided a chilling picture of the Antichrist. "The coming of the lawless one will be in accordance with the work of Satan displayed in all kinds of counterfeit miracles, signs and wonders, and in every sort of evil that deceives those who are perishing" (2 Thessalonians 2:9-10). The appearance of the Antichrist will be accompanied by a display of miracles unparalleled since the time of Jesus and the apostles.

Satan's power is limited. He is not all-powerful, nor is he all-knowing or omnipresent. But he still brings with him an array of supernatural abilities that dwarf the natural abilities of mere mortals. Satan will work to enhance the credibility of the Antichrist by bestowing on him seemingly miraculous powers. This latter-day superman will appear to have "powers far beyond those of mortal men."

What type of miracles will Satan use to enhance the credibility of the Antichrist? Paul does not say specifically, but he does suggest that the kinds of miracles will be many and varied. Since the Antichrist is trying to mimic the person and ministry of Jesus Christ, it is possible that some miracles will closely parallel those performed by Jesus when He was on earth.

Our world has abandoned the truth of God's Word. We live in a spiritually bankrupt society where only existential truth is accepted. "I'll believe it if I can see it or experience it." Yet the world is searching for something or someone to fill the spiritual void that only God can fill. Having rejected the Truth, people are vulnerable to a message that wraps a lie in human experience. Since the world has rejected the spiritual reality of demons, everyone will marvel at verifiable "miracles" that this world leader seems capable of performing. The miracles will be real, but the source of the Antichrist's power will be hidden from view.

Peace at Last?

The world searches desperately for peace apart from God. We want all the benefits without accepting any of the responsibilities. We look for a leader who will offer hope without asking us to acknowledge our sin. We want a New World Order—as long as that order meets our wants without impinging on our lifestyle. In short, we want a secular Jesus Christ who will bring in a godless millennium.

That leader could be just on the horizon. He will appear as the answer to the world's prayers—a man who can bring peace and prosperity to a world racked by pain. His actions will speak louder than his words as he—literally—does the impossible. "If I hadn't

seen it with my own eyes, I wouldn't have believed it"
will be a litany on the lips of his converts worldwide.
He will bring enforced peace to a war-weary world.

The world will be so mesmerized by his miracles
that his other actions will scarcely be noticed. His
world peace will be purchased by an unparalleled
increase in defense spending. Military might will be
his top priority. He may appear to wear a velvet glove,
but the glove only masks a fist of iron that will strike
against any who dare oppose him. The world will
wake up to his total control, but by then it will be too
late. People will be forced to pay homage to this evil
ruler because they know the consequences of disobedience. "Who is like the beast? Who can make war
against him?" (Revelation 13:4). In the end the man of
peace will turn out to be the "man of lawlessness."
But for most still on earth the discovery will come too
late.

CHAPTER FOURTEEN
BEAUTY ON THE BEAST

In the 1960s, children in the United States grew up watching "The Beverly Hillbillies," an improbable tale of a family of hillbillies who struck it rich and moved to California. The source of their wealth was the accidental discovery of oil on Jed Clampett's land. The world's demand for oil has the power to transform ordinary hillbillies into "Beverly Hillbillies."

The rags-to-riches story of Jed Clampett seems too contrived to be true, but it accurately mirrors the Persian Gulf of the past century. The discovery of oil transformed a group of bedouins into billionaires and changed the face of the Middle East. In the early 1900s Abdul Aziz Ibn Saud led his Wahabi tribe in conquest over other tribes in the Arabian Peninsula. By 1926 he proclaimed himself king, and in 1932 he named his kingdom Saudi Arabia. Much of his empire's interior was nothing but barren sand and rock. At any gathering of nations no one would have voted Saudi Arabia "most likely to succeed."

But in 1935 everything changed for the Al-Saud family and their desolate domain. That year American

geologists discovered Saudi Arabia's vast oil deposits.
Over the years estimates of the size of Saudi Arabia's
oil reserves continued to climb. Today Saudi Arabia's
proven oil reserves are estimated to be more than 250
billion barrels. One-fourth of the proven oil reserves
of the entire world lie within this one country.

Saudi Arabia, though the largest, is not the only Persian Gulf nation with a rags-to-riches story. Oil was
discovered in Iran and Iraq before it was found in
Saudi Arabia. The British first tapped Iran's oil
reserves in 1908. Less than twenty years later they
struck oil in Iraq. Just after the discovery of oil in
Saudi Arabia, large oil deposits were found in the tiny
country of Kuwait. Saudi Arabia, Iraq, and Kuwait
together account for 50 percent of the world's proven
oil reserves.

Give Me Oil in My Lamp

The world is addicted to fossil fuels, and OPEC
remains the world's largest supplier. As we
approach the year 2000, oil will supply even more
of the world's energy needs. And OPEC will
increase its market share. "Demand for OPEC oil
grew from 15 million barrels a day in 1986 to over
20 million barrels just three years later. By 2000, it
will easily top 25 million barrels daily."[1] The
United States remains the largest user of oil worldwide, and its own oil reserves continue to decline.
But instead of increasing its exploration for oil, the
U.S. is turning more to the countries of the Middle
East to supply its needs.

Yet in spite of the world's growing dependence on

Middle East oil, many are predicting that oil prices will actually fall during the coming decade. Competition between OPEC countries and the inability of OPEC to control its production are cited as reasons for this optimistic prediction: "OPEC is not very good at throttling back production to keep prices up when their market is glutted. They will not get any better at it in the 1990s."[2] Can we be assured of abundant, cheap oil for the remainder of this century?

Saddam's Surprise

The world has an abundant supply of oil that should last well into the next century. The problem is that more than half of the supply sits under the sands of the most politically unstable region of the world. Any predictions that do not consider the political and religious instability of the Middle East are doomed to fail. In the mid-1970s no one predicted the overthrow of the Shah of Iran by Ayatollah Khomeini and his religious fundamentalists. In early 1990 no one believed that Saddam Hussein would dare invade Kuwait. Yet both events did take place, and they had the potential to disrupt oil supplies to the West.

Saddam Hussein's invasion of Kuwait proved particularly worrisome because of the swiftness of his actions and the potential damage to the world's supply of oil. Overnight Hussein doubled the amount of oil under his control to 25 percent of the world's proven reserves. But more troubling were reports that he planned to send his forces on into Saudi Arabia. The specter of one man controlling half the world's oil supply sent oil prices skyrocketing and pushed President Bush into launching Operation Desert Shield.

Saddam Hussein did not succeed, but he came perilously close to creating a one-man monopoly over much of the world's oil. And that raises a frightening question for a world that can't wean itself off oil. What if one man could control Iraq, Kuwait, and Saudi Arabia? What if Saddam Hussein had not stopped at Kuwait but had continued on into Saudi Arabia before our forces could react?

The Allied coalition stopped Saddam Hussein and forced him from Kuwait, but he is still in control of Iraq. Should the United States ever weaken in its resolve, what's to stop Saddam Hussein or his successor from moving again against his neighbors to the south? Old grudges die slowly in the Middle East, and Saddam Hussein has a score to settle with the ruling families of Kuwait and Saudi Arabia. Should the United States ever be unable or unwilling to come to the aid of her Arab allies, Iraq's troops could again pour over the border.

A one-man cartel controlling the oil of the Middle East would disrupt the world's economy. Two results would become immediately evident. First, this individual would cut production, raise the price of oil, and reap the profits. Second, those countries heavily dependent on oil would feel the economic pressure of being held hostage to this tyrant from the Middle East. Economically he could control the industrial nations and influence their actions and policies. Europe would be especially hard hit since it is so dependent on oil from the Middle East.

When Beauty Rides the Beast

The Apostle John pictures just such a scene in Revelation 17–18. John describes the complex relationship that will exist in the end times between the Antichrist and a ruler who lives in Babylon. Using language from the prophet Daniel, John describes the Antichrist and his empire as a "beast." This is the same beast John described in Revelation 13:4 as the end-time world power that would dominate all other nations militarily ("Who is like the beast? Who can make war against him?").

But something is drastically wrong in Revelation 17. The beast might be the military master of the world, but someone seems to exert control over the beast. "There I saw a woman sitting on a scarlet beast" (17:3). The angel announces to John, "Why are you astonished? I will explain to you the mystery of the woman and of the beast she rides" (17:7). John's vision suggests that this woman will in some way ride on, or exert control over, the final world ruler. But how can this be?

In chapter 10 we explored the identity of this woman named Babylon. God identifies the woman as the literal city of Babylon. This city, located fifty miles south of present-day Baghdad, is now being rebuilt by Saddam Hussein. Somehow the ruler of Babylon will exert control over the Antichrist through much of the final seven-year period of his rule.

The Antichrist does not enjoy his relationship with Babylon, but he puts up with it for a period of time. Finally, however, he launches "Operation Desert Storm II" to eliminate this thorn in his side. "The beast and the ten horns you saw will hate the prostitute. They will bring her to ruin and leave her naked; they will eat her flesh and burn her with fire" (17:16). Using his superior military forces, the Antichrist will ultimately destroy the nation that has caused him such trouble.

The Bible does not say specifically how the revived city of Babylon will control the Antichrist and his empire, but John does write that Babylon's influence will be commercial and economic. When Babylon falls, those involved in trade and commerce will mourn. "The merchants of the earth will weep and mourn over her because no one buys their cargoes any more" (18:11). Even the ship captains grieve over the city that brought them such wealth. "Woe! Woe, O great city, where all who had ships on the sea became rich through her wealth!" (18:19).

Babylon will exert economic control over the Antichrist and his empire. The Bible does not provide any details on what will be involved in this economic control, but oil remains the most likely suspect. Since Saddam Hussein's invasion, it is much easier to imagine one individual controlling the oil wealth of the Middle East and using his billions to complete the reconstruction of the city of Babylon. This ruler will play a dominant role in the world because of his control over oil. Truly his empire, centered in the new city of Babylon, will be "the great city that rules over the kings of the earth" (Revelation 17:18).

The Antichrist will be the dominant military power in the world. Yet he will still have weaknesses and limitations. One serious handicap will be his dependence on oil from the Middle East. He will control the world's strongest army, but his army needs oil to operate. He will find himself hampered by the one resource over which he lacks control.

As the Antichrist rises in Europe, another ruler will gain control of the oil wealth in the Middle East. This ruler will force the price of oil to go up, and the price increase will send hundreds of billions of dollars into his coffers. Much of the money will be used to enlarge and beautify his new capital—the rebuilt city of Babylon. From his new city on the Euphrates he will oversee the rise and fall of nations around the world simply by controlling the price and availability of oil.

In 1990 the world waited six months until the Allied forces felt strong enough to respond militarily to Saddam Hussein's invasion of Kuwait. Had Saddam Hussein gone into Saudi Arabia, the response time could have taken much longer. In the end times the Antichrist will not be able to respond as rapidly for two reasons. First, he will be fighting other, more pressing, battles elsewhere. Second, he will not be able to garrison his forces in Saudi Arabia because it will already be under the control of the king from Babylon.

Only after putting down other pockets of resistance will the Antichrist turn his army toward Babylon. Attacking from the north, his forces will descend on Babylon. "A nation from the north will attack her and lay waste her land" (Jeremiah 50:3). One of the Antichrist's last campaigns during the seven-year period is to destroy the man and the city that have caused him such difficulty. The world leader believes he is defeating the nation that has prevented him from wielding absolute power. But instead of accomplishing his objectives, he is merely carrying out the plans of God.

Revelation 17 shows the final relationship between the Middle East and the empire of the Antichrist. God's vision to John is of two end-time powers that will control the world. Babylon's power is economic and monetary. She becomes rich supplying the needs of the world. In doing so she dominates the world economically. The Antichrist's empire is military and industrial. He crushes nations that stand in his way, and he exerts political and military control over all others. His only weakness is his empire's dependence on Babylon's oil. His ultimate "solution" to the problem is to attack and destroy the nation causing him such grief. Once Babylon is destroyed, all roads lead to Armageddon.

CHAPTER FIFTEEN
DESTINATION: ARMAGEDDON

The bus crawls up the narrow pass that slices through Mount Carmel. On either side stand the mountains that make up the Carmel range. Like silent sentinels they guard this gateway on the International Highway that led from Egypt to Mesopotamia. Countless caravans and conquerors have made the journey up the pass as they rode over the well-worn road that linked the two great civilizations of the ancient Middle East.

Today our bus, appropriately called a *merkabah*—the Hebrew word for chariot—reenacts the frightening ascent up this pass recorded by Pharaoh Thutmose III nearly 3,500 years before. His military advisers argued for using any alternative to the route we were on: "What is it like to go [on] this [road] which becomes (so) narrow? . . . Let our victorious lord proceed on the one of [them] which is [satisfactory to] his heart, (but) do not make us go on that difficult road!"[1] Thutmose III ignored his advisers and drove his chariots up this highway to attack a coalition of Canaanite cities that had rebelled against Egypt. Our destination is the same one selected by Thutmose III—Megiddo.

As we break through the mountains, the Jezreel Valley stretches out before us. On our left stands the ancient city of Megiddo. The ruins of the ancient city sit on a hill guarding the highway as it opens up into this vast valley. The hill has grown higher over time as the successive conquerors of Megiddo rebuilt the city on the ruins of the previous inhabitants. Archaeologists have discovered twenty-four separate layers of occupation on Megiddo—a mute reminder of the violent history of this strategic city.

As we walk through the gate complex built by King Solomon, I realize that Israel's wisest king understood the importance of Megiddo. The compiler of the book of Kings paused in his description of Solomon to note that King Solomon fortified his capital city and three other key cities in his empire—"Hazor, Megiddo and Gezer" (1 Kings 9:15). Scholars still debate the specific function of several large buildings constructed by the nation of Israel on the site. Whether the buildings served as stables or storehouses, they show us that Megiddo was a major regional center in Israel.

Our group gathers at the northeast corner of the tell to look out over the Jezreel Valley. Through the haze in the distance, Mount Tabor rises from the valley floor. Just to our right, in a trench gouged into the side of the tell, stands an ancient Canaanite altar exposed by archaeologists. The altar reminds us that Megiddo's significance predates Solomon by 1,500 years. Megiddo served as the nerve center for the Jezreel Valley long before any Israelites walked through her gates.

Megiddo's strategic location in the Jezreel Valley at

the mouth of the road through Mount Carmel caused
the city much grief. The city suffered sieges and
attacks, and countless armies gathered outside her
gates. Solomon, the last king who ruled over the
united empire of Israel, fortified the city against
attack. Josiah, the last good king of Judah, died at
Megiddo trying to stop the army of Egypt from going
to fight against the Babylonians. "While Josiah was
king, Pharaoh Neco king of Egypt went up to the
Euphrates River to help the king of Assyria. King
Josiah marched out to meet him in battle, but Neco
faced him and killed him at Megiddo" (2 Kings
23:29).

The hill of Megiddo, in Hebrew *har megiddo*, symbolized the place where armies assembled for war.
The Jezreel Valley provided ample room for gathering
an army and conducting maneuvers. Control of the
pass through Mount Carmel gave the city military
importance. Is it any wonder that when God gathers
the Antichrist and his army to Israel for the final
battle, the armies will assemble at the hill of Megiddo,
which transliterated into Greek is Armageddon?
"Then they gathered the kings together to the place
that in Hebrew is called Armageddon" (Revelation
16:16).

Is Armageddon the End of the World?

Opponents of the nuclear arms race warned against
Armageddon—the sudden and complete annihilation
of life on earth in a great nuclear holocaust. They used
the term *Armageddon* to describe the last great war on

earth that would destroy humanity. But is this what
the Bible describes as the Battle of Armageddon?

The Bible never pictures Armageddon as the final
battle in world history, nor does the Bible associate
Armageddon with the end of the world. In fact, the
Bible doesn't even say specifically that a battle will be
fought at Armageddon. God describes Armageddon as
the staging area for the armies of the world as they prepare to oppose Jesus Christ when He returns to earth.
A careful look at Revelation 16 gives the sequence of
events just before the second coming of Jesus to earth.
Included in those events is the gathering at Armageddon.

In Revelation 16, God pours out His final bowls of
judgment on the earth. These judgments occur in the
last days and weeks before the second coming of
Jesus to earth. The next-to-last judgment is the sixth
bowl that the angel pours out on the earth (16:12-16).
The Euphrates River that snakes through the Middle
East from Turkey to the Persian Gulf will dry up. God
removes this barrier "to prepare the way for the kings
from the East." The world powers will come together,
and the drying up of the Euphrates hastens their
arrival.

With the physical barriers eliminated, Satan sends
his demonic messengers to summon all the nations.
"They are spirits of demons performing miraculous
signs, and they go out to the kings of the whole world,
to gather them for the battle on the great day of God
Almighty" (16:14). The armies are coming for battle,
but whom do they come to fight? Many have thought
that the armies are coming to fight each other. As a

result they described the gathering of the armies at Armageddon as the final great battle of the world. But the Bible does not say that these armies are coming to fight one another. Could they have another enemy in view?

Satan and his human henchmen send the demons to summon the armies. The armies come as allies, not enemies. Armageddon serves more as a staging ground than a battlefield. Other passages in the Bible suggest that the final battle between the earthly armies and Jesus will occur at Jerusalem instead of in northern Israel at Armageddon. Armageddon serves as the rallying point for the remaining armies of earth to join their leader in his final campaign of conquest.

The Antichrist's Final Days

The gathering of the armies at Armageddon is not the climax of world history. One final bowl of judgment must still be poured out on the earth before Jesus returns to claim His throne. The Apostle John pictures the final judgment of God in Revelation 16:17-21. As the judgment from this final bowl spills onto the earth, the voice from God's temple in heaven cries, "It is done!" This judgment will complete God's program of punishment and set the stage for the coming of Jesus.

The final bowl of judgment brings two types of terrors. First, God will send a series of catastrophic calamities on the earth:

> There came flashes of lightning, rumblings, peals of thunder and a severe earthquake. No earth-

quake like it has ever occurred since man has
been on earth, so tremendous was the quake. . . .
Every island fled away and the mountains could
not be found. From the sky huge hailstones of
about a hundred pounds each fell upon men.
(Revelation 16:18, 20-21)

The world will convulse in a final spasm of anguish as
God turns the forces of nature against its inhabitants.

The second judgment from this final bowl falls on
the city of Babylon: "God remembered Babylon the
Great and gave her the cup filled with the wine of the
fury of his wrath" (16:19). In the next two chapters of
the book of Revelation the Apostle John describes
how Babylon will be destroyed by the Antichrist and
his army. In the previous chapter we saw that the Antichrist will be dependent on the ruler of Babylon. The
summoning of the armies to Armageddon could be
the prelude to "Operation Desert Storm II." The
armies that gather travel to Babylon to destroy the city
that has caused the Antichrist such grief. Following
this destruction of Babylon, the Antichrist's army
returns to Israel to destroy the Jews. Then Jesus Christ
returns to earth.

Do we have any other indication in Scripture that
Armageddon might be the prelude to a series of last
battles and not the final battle itself? The prophet Daniel offers a glimpse of the final days of the Antichrist
that might give us a clue. In Daniel 11:36-45 the
prophet pictures the career of this man of sin. In 11:36-
39 Daniel describes the Antichrist's rise to power as
he exalts himself and honors "a god of fortresses."

These verses capture the essence of the Antichrist's strategy during most of the final seven-year period—military might and self-promotion.

But beginning in 11:40 Daniel focuses specifically on the events "at the time of the end." In these verses Daniel describes the final movements and battles of the Antichrist and his army. In verse 41 the Antichrist "will also invade the Beautiful Land [Israel]." Some have felt that this invasion must be in the middle of the final seven-year period when the Antichrist goes to the temple in Jerusalem and proclaims himself to be God. But the Antichrist's arrival at the middle of the Tribulation catches everyone off guard because of his earlier peace treaty with Israel. That event happens so suddenly that those working in the field won't even have time to return to their houses before fleeing in panic (Matthew 24:15-21). The invasion in Daniel 11:40-41 will be known in advance because the Antichrist will come "with chariots and cavalry and a great fleet of ships."

I believe the invasion of "the Beautiful Land" in Daniel 11:41 is parallel to the gathering of the armies at Armageddon. The Antichrist summons an "International Task Force" to eliminate the final pockets of resistance to his domination of the world. They gather at Armageddon and move south toward Egypt and Africa. "He will extend his power over many countries; Egypt will not escape. He will gain control of the treasures of gold and silver and all the riches of Egypt, with the Libyans and Nubians in submission" (11:42-43). The armies attack Egypt and her African

allies and force them to surrender. The Antichrist's
southern flank is now secure.

Unfortunately, one victory brings another rebellion.
"Reports from the east and the north will alarm him,
and he will set out in a great rage to destroy and annihilate many" (11:44). What are the reports from the
east and the north, and who will be annihilated? If
Daniel is describing the last days of the Antichrist's
rule, the disturbing news could come from Babylon.
Perhaps Babylon's ruler resented the destruction of
his Arab brothers and threatened to cut off the supply
of oil, or perhaps he "saw the handwriting on the
wall" and reacted to protect himself from the attack he
knew would come. Whatever the reason, the news
alarmed the Antichrist, and he sent his army off on
another campaign of destruction and terror. Babylon
would be "east and north" of Egypt, and the book of
Revelation predicts that Babylon will be the final city
to fall to the Antichrist before Jesus returns to earth.

After taking care of the problem "from the east and
the north," the Antichrist will set out on his final campaign. "He will pitch his royal tents between the seas
at the beautiful holy mountain" (11:45). Daniel does
not name the location where the Antichrist and his
army camp, but he provides enough details for us to
know where this army will strike last. The two "seas"
are the Mediterranean Sea and the Dead Sea. The Antichrist ends up in Israel. The "beautiful holy mountain"
between these two seas is the city of Jerusalem. The
final phase of the Antichrist's campaign of destruction
could be called "Operation Jerusalem"!

Operation Jerusalem

Using Israel as the beachhead, the Antichrist sends his army south to control Egypt and Africa and then north and east to destroy Babylon and control the rest of the Middle East. Having successfully eliminated these "thorns in his side," the Antichrist turns to the enemy he has tried to destroy for the past three-and-a-half years. Operation Jerusalem has as its goals the complete destruction of the capital of Israel and the elimination of every Jew still alive in the land of Israel.

The prophet Joel described this final battle of the ages. In poetic language he pictured the nations planning for the final attack against Jerusalem.

> Proclaim this among the nations: Prepare for war! Rouse the warriors! Let all the fighting men draw near and attack. Beat your plowshares into swords and your pruning hooks into spears. Let the weakling say, "I am strong!" Come quickly, all you nations from every side, and assemble there. Bring down your warriors, O LORD! Let the nations be roused; let them advance into the Valley of Jehoshaphat, for there I will sit to judge all the nations on every side. (Joel 3:9-12)

The final battle against Israel will come as the nations gather at the Valley of Jehoshaphat—probably the Kidron Valley that runs on the east side of Jerusalem between the city and the Mount of Olives.

Zechariah also zeroed in on this final battle against Jerusalem. "I will gather all the nations to Jerusalem to fight against it; the city will be captured, the houses ransacked, and the women raped. Half of the city will go into exile, but the rest of the people will not be taken from the city" (Zechariah 14:2). How do we know that this is the final attack against Jerusalem and not another battle in history? Zechariah gives the answer in the next few verses.

> Then the LORD will go out and fight against those nations, as he fights in the day of battle. On that day his feet will stand on the Mount of Olives, east of Jerusalem, and the Mount of Olives will be split in two from east to west, forming a great valley, with half of the mountain moving north and half moving south. You will flee by my mountain valley, for it will extend to Azel. . . . Then the LORD my God will come, and all the holy ones with him. (Zechariah 14:3-5)

The attack against Jerusalem described by Zechariah only ends when Jesus returns to earth to rescue His people.

The King Is Coming!

Armageddon is not the final battle on earth. In fact, Armageddon is technically not even a battle. The name describes the broad valley where the armies will first gather for their final campaign. They then travel to Egypt to subdue Africa and to Babylon to destroy the city that has exercised control over the Antichrist throughout the seven-year period. Finally the army comes back to Jerusalem to put an end to the people of Israel.

Daniel, Joel, and Zechariah identify Jerusalem as the site where the final battle between the Antichrist and Christ will occur. All three predict that God will intervene in history on behalf of His people and will destroy the Antichrist's army at Jerusalem. Zechariah predicts that the battle will end when the Messiah returns to earth and His feet touch down on the Mount of Olives. This battle concludes with the second coming of Jesus to earth. But how ferocious will the final battle be between the Antichrist and Christ?

The Apostle John presents the actual battle in Revelation 19:11-21. As the battle begins, it looks to the world like it will turn into the "heavyweight battle of all eternity." John first introduces the "fighter in the white trunks"—Jesus Christ. As heaven opens up, John describes the awesome majesty of Jesus returning to earth with the armies of heaven following him (19:14). Jesus is the defending champion, and He is wearing the title "King of kings and Lord of lords" (19:16).

The scene shifts, and an angel summons all the birds of earth to gather for the fight. These feathery friends will observe "the climax of all battles" as they watch the best army on earth fight the army from heaven. The birds are invited to feast on the carcasses that will cover the battlefield following the conflict.

Then John introduces the "fighter in the black trunks." "The beast and the kings of the earth and their armies gathered together to make war against the rider on the horse and his army" (19:19). The Antichrist and his army represent all the might the world can muster. They have come to Jerusalem, and they will be the final challenge to Jesus as He returns to earth to claim His crown.

We settle down in our front-row seats expecting to watch the greatest fight ever held. The opponents are the champions in their respective divisions. The Antichrist is the best Satan has to offer, and he comes representing the evil empire that controls the world. Christ is the best God the Father has to offer, and He comes as Savior and Sovereign who has God's authority to rule the world. The bell sounds and the fighters step toward the center of the ring. And with one punch the contest is decided!

> But the beast was captured, and with him the false prophet who had performed the miraculous signs on his behalf. . . . The two of them were thrown alive into the fiery lake of burning sulfur. The rest of them were killed with the sword that came out of the mouth of the rider on the horse, and all the birds gorged themselves on their flesh. (Revelation 19:20-21)

The battle is over before it even begins.

The Battle of Armageddon—actually at Jerusalem—is the most anticlimactic battle in history. As John described the armies mustered on both sides, we expect to witness some epic struggle between good and evil. Yet no matter how mighty someone on earth is, that individual is no match for the power of God.

The prophet Isaiah described how the greatest power mustered on earth compares to the power of God: "Surely the nations are like a drop in a bucket;

they are regarded as dust on the scales. . . . Before him
all the nations are as nothing; they are regarded by
him as worthless and less than nothing" (Isaiah 40:15,
17). Compared to the power of God, the awesomeness
of the Antichrist and his army quickly fades.

The Antichrist and his assistant are captured and
cast immediately into eternal punishment—an igno-
minious end for the man who claimed to be God. The
vast army gathered against Jerusalem falls dead when
Jesus utters but a word out of His mouth. They don't
even have the opportunity to fire their weapons. What
began as the gathering at Armageddon ends as a lopsided victory for Jesus Christ. He retains His eternal
title: "King of kings and Lord of lords."

PART FOUR

PROPHECY:
HOW DO TOMORROW'S HEADLINES MEET TODAY'S NEEDS?

All truth might be God's truth, but some truth is more practical and relevant than other truth. The fact that the ratio of the circumference of a circle to its diameter is an irrational number—whose value to five decimal places is 3.14159—is a truth of life. So is the fact that the force of gravity on earth causes bodies to fall toward the center of the earth with uniform acceleration. But someone stretching out on the edge of his roof trying to paint the upper reaches of his house is probably more concerned about the effects of the second truth than the first.

In the Bible, God's prophets pulled back the veil of time to announce God's future program for His creation. Much of what they predicted came to pass during the first coming of Jesus to earth. But many events await a future fulfillment that will culminate when Jesus returns to earth a second time to establish His kingdom. Predictive prophecy is part of the truth of God's Word.

Yet many people prefer not to study those portions of the Bible that describe future events. Why do they shy away? Two main reasons surface: reliability and relevance.

Reliability. How can I know for sure that God did intend to predict the future? Many sincere Christians disagree about Bible prophecy. Can I be certain that the events described in the Bible are literal events that will take place? If I am not sure, I will "play it safe" and only study those parts of the Bible that I'm sure I can understand.

Relevance. Even if the Bible does predict the future, so what? Since prophecy describes what will happen on earth after I'm gone, of what practical bene-fit is it to me today? I would rather study those por-tions of the Bible that tell me how to live for Jesus now. Why study about the "Sweet By and By" when I'm struggling in the dismal here and now?

Did God really predict the future? If He did, does it have any practical benefit for me today? Western civi-lization's preoccupation with reliability and relevance provide two formidable foes against focusing on Bible prophecy. Does the Bible provide answers to these questions? I believe the answer is yes. This final sec-tion will show how tomorrow's headlines can meet today's needs.

CHAPTER SIXTEEN
DOES GOD REALLY PREDICT THE FUTURE?

What is the purpose of the Old Testament [pro-
phetic] material? Is it to provide a blueprint of
world history for centuries to come or is it to
make preparation for the coming of the Messiah
in and through the life and history of the nation
of Israel? Is its purpose to reveal events surrounding the second coming of Jesus or to prepare for
the events of his first coming as God brings to
fruition his plan of redeeming man from his sin?
Again, the latter alternative in each case is the
correct answer.[1]

Blueprint or broad outline? Did God really intend to
predict future events? Or are we, as the above writer
claims, reading into the Bible when we try to discern
His program for the ages? This issue cuts to the heart
of Bible prophecy, and it affects how we interpret the
Bible. Anyone who believes the Bible is the Word of
God must address this issue. Unfortunately, many are
afraid to examine the issue of Bible prophecy.
    Christians do not want to misuse the Bible, and

some feel very uncomfortable as they tread across the unfamiliar terrain of Old and New Testament prophecy. Many choose simply to detour those regions of the Bible that force them to ask whether the Bible predicts the future. But to do so takes away some of the very words given by God "for teaching, rebuking, correcting and training in righteousness" (2 Timothy 3:16). There must be a better way.

Believe It or Not!

In the spring of 1990 I took my son, Ben, on a trip to San Antonio. After I spoke at Dallas Seminary's extension class, we toured the city. We visited the River Walk and the Alamo, but we still had some extra time. So I asked Ben what he wanted to see. Pointing across the street, Ben said he wanted to visit "Ripley's Believe It or Not." We spent several hours staring at matchstick houses, shrunken heads, and unusual epitaphs!

Robert Ripley started his cartoon feature "Believe It or Not" in 1918. He featured the odd, the strange, and the unusual. But as bizarre and unbelievable as some items seemed, they were still true. Perhaps the lesson to be learned from Ripley is that sometimes truth is stranger than fiction.

Can we believe that when God directed His prophets to pen the Scriptures, He enabled them to predict the future? Is there some objective way to test the predictive element of the Bible? Does the Bible itself provide any clues that show us whether God intended to predict the future when He gave us His Word? Thankfully, the Bible does provide an answer.

God Claims to Predict the Future

The prophet Isaiah lived in a time of political and moral upheaval. God called him to be a prophet the year King Uzziah died. Uzziah's fifty-two-year reign over Judah was a time of unparalleled peace and prosperity. The Bible identified Uzziah as a king who "did what was right in the eyes of the LORD" (2 Kings 15:3). Yet Uzziah, in one foolish act, marred his otherwise sterling record of service. In pride he usurped the authority of the priests and offered incense on the altar in the temple. God struck the king with leprosy and forced Uzziah to live the final decade of his life in seclusion and isolation. Sometime during 740–739 B.C., Uzziah died.

Over the next decade Isaiah watched Judah decline. The country went from being a strong nation under King Uzziah to little more than a puppet nation under King Uzziah's grandson, Ahaz. Ahaz surrendered Judah's independence to Assyria to buy protection from Judah's enemies to the north. Assyria forced Judah to make yearly payments for this "protection." Judah surrendered her sovereignty as Assyria looted her treasury.

King Hezekiah followed his father, Ahaz, to the throne. When Assyria's king died, Hezekiah (along with the kings of several other countries) declared his independence and stopped paying the money extorted by Assyria. The new king of Assyria, Sennacherib, had his hands full at home securing his throne from potential rivals. But by 703 B.C. Sennacherib sent out his army to recapture those nations that had rebelled.

It took two years, but by 701 B.C. the Assyrian juggernaut rolled into Judah.

Isaiah gives a grim summary of Sennacherib's attack: "In the fourteenth year of King Hezekiah's reign, Sennacherib king of Assyria attacked all the fortified cities of Judah and captured them. Then the king of Assyria sent his field commander with a large army from Lachish to King Hezekiah at Jerusalem" (Isaiah 36:1-2). Sennacherib provides us with an even more colorful analysis of his campaign. "As to Hezekiah, the Jew, he did not submit to my yoke, I laid siege to forty-six of his strong cities, walled forts and to the countless small villages in their vicinity, and conquered them. . . . Himself I made a prisoner in Jerusalem, his royal residence, like a bird in a cage."[2]

King Hezekiah received Sennacherib's ultimatum and understood the awful consequences of trying to resist the powerful Assyrian army. Yet Hezekiah responded in a way that marks him as a true man of faith. "Hezekiah received the letter from the messengers and read it. Then he went up to the temple of the LORD and spread it out before the LORD" (Isaiah 37:14). Hezekiah wanted God to see the boastful words of the pagan king. He then asked God to do the impossible and to intervene for Judah: "Now, O LORD our God, deliver us from his hand, so that all kingdoms on earth may know that you alone, O LORD, are God" (37:20).

God listened to Hezekiah's prayer. "Then the angel of the LORD went out and put to death a hundred and eighty-five thousand men in the Assyrian camp" (37:36). Sennacherib awoke to find that God had done what no human army had been able to do. The mighty army of Assyria buried its dead, gathered its weapons, concluded a hastily drawn peace treaty, and withdrew from Judah. Judah again began paying tribute to Assyria, but Hezekiah remained king over Judah. He was the only ruler who rebelled against Assyria and remained on his throne as king.

Hezekiah's great "victory" over the Assyrians brought him much recognition, but it also sealed Judah's ultimate doom. The former king of Babylon, Merodach-Baladan, sent an envoy to Hezekiah. Though they "officially" came to wish Hezekiah well on his recovery from a recent illness, they really wanted to know how he had defeated the king of Assyria and managed to remain on his throne. Merodach-Baladan had not been so lucky. Sennacherib attacked Babylon in 703 B.C. and forced Merodach-Baladan to flee. Merodach-Baladan spent the rest of his life trying—unsuccessfully—to regain his throne.

One can almost hear the messengers fawning over Hezekiah. "We are so happy that you are doing well physically. The world needs strong leaders like you who can stand up to the evil Assyrians." Then they lowered their voices and revealed the real purpose for their visit. "Hezekiah, our lord, Merodach-Baladan, is still struggling to regain his throne at Babylon. We would be interested in forming an alliance with you against King Sennacherib of Assyria. But tell us, Hezekiah, how were you able to chase the Assyrians from your land? How did you defeat the Assyrian army?"

What an excellent opportunity for Hezekiah to point toward the temple in Jerusalem and to tell these messengers about the God of Israel! But overcome by pride, the king introduced them to the glories of Hezekiah rather than the God of Israel. "Hezekiah received the envoys gladly and showed them what was in his storehouses—the silver, the gold, the spices, the fine oil, his entire armory and everything found among his treasuries. There was nothing in his palace or in all his kingdom that Hezekiah did not show them" (Isaiah 39:2).

Hezekiah's pitiful display of pride took place in 700 B.C. God sent the prophet Isaiah with a prediction of judgment that would come on Judah because of Hezekiah's foolish actions:

> The time will surely come when everything in your palace, and all that your fathers have stored up until this day, will be carried off to Babylon. Nothing will be left, says the LORD. And some of your descendants, your own flesh and blood who will be born to you, will be taken away, and they will become eunuchs in the palace of the king of Babylon. (Isaiah 39:6-7)

Here is a definite prediction against the land of Judah. Isaiah is claiming, on behalf of God, that the Babylonians will succeed where the Assyrians have failed. Babylon will attack and loot the city of Jerusalem. God had spared Hezekiah's life, but Hezekiah's own physical descendants would be dragged away to Babylon.

How was Isaiah's prediction fulfilled? Was his message a blueprint for Judah's future or just a broad outline? Almost a century after Isaiah penned his words,

God fulfilled them exactly as Isaiah had predicted.
King Nebuchadnezzar of Babylon attacked Jerusalem.
Three times his army entered the city. Each time they
carried away hostages and booty. The prophet Daniel
specifically alludes to Isaiah's prediction. Besides
plundering the temple, Nebuchadnezzar also captured
"Israelites from the royal family" (Daniel 1:3) and carried them back to Babylon—just as Isaiah had predicted a century earlier!

Isaiah was so certain that Judah would go into captivity in Babylon that he spent the remainder of his
book speaking to those people who would be carried
away. Though writing about 700 B.C., Isaiah makes a
number of predictions about the future. In several of
these prophecies God claims that He is predicting the
future. Read what Isaiah writes and decide for yourself whether or not God intended to predict the future.

God announces that He will predict the future to
prove that He alone is God. Only the true God who is
in control of the universe has knowledge of the future.
God turns to people surrounded by false, pagan gods
and says, "Here is a test to prove that I alone am God.
I will write down events in the days of Isaiah the
prophet so that when they occur in the future you will
know that I predicted them in advance." God claims
to predict the future, and He claims that these predictions are proof of His deity: "Bring in your idols to tell
us what is going to happen. Tell us what the former
things were, so that we may consider them and know
their final outcome. Or declare to us the things to
come, tell us what the future holds, so we may know
that you are gods" (Isaiah 41:22-23).

Just a few chapters later Isaiah again issues God's challenge to any "wanna-be" gods that people might put forth as potential rivals to the God of Israel: "Who then is like me? Let him proclaim it. Let him declare and lay out before me what has happened since I established my ancient people, and what is yet to come— yes, let him foretell what will come" (44:7). God claims that He can and does predict the future. And He makes His predictions so that—when they occur just as He predicted—people will know that He alone is God.

God claims to predict the future. But what specifically did He predict in this portion of Isaiah? The most remarkable prediction occurs in Isaiah 45:

> This is what the LORD says to his anointed, to Cyrus, whose right hand I take hold of to subdue nations before him and to strip kings of their armor, to open doors before him so that gates will not be shut. . . . For the sake of Jacob my servant, of Israel my chosen, I summon you by name and bestow on you a title of honor, though you do not acknowledge me. I am the LORD, and there is no other; apart from me there is no God. (Isaiah 45:1, 4-5)

In Isaiah 45 God predicted that someone named Cyrus would rescue the Jews from Babylon. More than 160 years after Isaiah's anouncement, Cyrus, king of the Medo-Persian Empire, defeated the Babylonians and issued a decree allowing the Jews to return to the land of Israel!

This prophecy boggles the mind. In a section where God claims to predict the future, He provides an example of the type of predictions He can make. Not only did God predict that Judah would fall to the Babylonians (which happened a century after Isaiah's prediction); God also announced that Judah would be rescued from Babylon by a conqueror who would be named Cyrus. God's predictions were specific and detailed, and they came to pass exactly as He said they would.

Others Believed the Bible's Prophecies

The story is told of the rural community that was experiencing a severe drought. Farmers watched helplessly as the corn crop shriveled under the unrelenting sun. The ground cracked, and dust devils swirled through the fields. Weeks passed with scarcely a cloud in the sky. As concern deepened into panic, the little church that served the community declared a day of prayer to ask God for relief from the drought. The appointed day arrived, and the community came to the church to pray. Farmers and field hands sat beside bankers and businessmen as the town united in asking God for rain. One young girl walked into the church clutching an umbrella. "Why are you carrying an umbrella?" some friends asked in jest. "Well, we are praying for rain!" responded the girl. She had the faith to believe God could accomplish what He was being asked to do.

God claimed to foretell the future throughout the Bible, but is there any evidence that individuals believed God could do what He had predicted? Did they understand God's promises to be a blueprint for the future, or were His words nothing more than a vague allusion? One way to answer the question is to see how other Bible writers understood God's predictions. Let's visit with some individuals and ask them how they interpret Bible prophecy.

Our first visit is with Daniel, trusted adviser in the royal court of Babylon. Daniel served as an adviser to King Nebuchadnezzar. Captured and deported to Babylon as a young man, Daniel rose to this place of prominence because of his unswerving faithfulness to God. He embodied the character traits of a godly leader.

Though Daniel spent most of his life far from Jerusalem, he was never far from his God. The few personal glimpses we have of Daniel reveal a man of prayer who oriented his life around God. Even his enemies noticed his life-style: "We will never find any basis for charges against this man Daniel unless it has something to do with the law of his God" (Daniel 6:5). Daniel read, studied, and obeyed the Word of God.

Late in his life we catch one memorable glimpse of Daniel's disciplined life of prayer and Bible study. In Daniel 9 the prophet made a profound discovery in the book of Jeremiah that pushed him to his knees in prayer. What had Daniel found in Jeremiah that had such an impact on his life? He discovered a specific prediction made by God.

Jeremiah announced that Jerusalem would be destroyed by Babylon. In his climactic announcement of judgment against Jerusalem, Jeremiah predicted, "This whole country will become a desolate wasteland, and these nations will serve the king of Babylon seventy years" (Jeremiah 25:11). Jerusalem would go into captivity in Babylon for seventy years! Only after this time of judgment would God allow His people to return to the land of Israel.

Daniel had been among the first group of Jews carried into captivity by the Babylonians in 605 B.C. The Jews remained prisoners of the Babylonians until Babylon fell to Cyrus the Medo-Persian in 539 B.C. In Daniel 9:1-2 the prophet notes that he was reading the book of Jeremiah "in the first year of Darius son of Xerxes (a Mede by descent), who was made ruler over the Babylonian kingdom." Whether Darius is another name for Cyrus or a subruler appointed by Cyrus is not clear. But what is clear is that Daniel was studying the book of Jeremiah about 538–537 B.C. Daniel had been in Babylon almost sixty-nine years!

As Daniel read Jeremiah's message, he came to God's prediction that the Jews would be in Babylon for seventy years. How did Daniel interpret this prophecy? Did he see it as a specific blueprint showing the exact amount of time for Jerusalem's desolation at the hand of Babylon? Or was Jeremiah's message just a vague warning that Jerusalem would suffer?

> I, Daniel, understood from the Scriptures, according to the word of the LORD given to Jeremiah the prophet, that the desolation of Jerusalem would last seventy years. So I turned to the LORD God and pleaded with him in prayer and petition, in fasting, and in sackcloth and ashes. (Daniel 9:2-3)

Daniel read God's prediction given by Jeremiah. And he understood it as an exact prediction of the number of years that the city of Jerusalem and the people of Judah would suffer at the hands of the Babylonians. Daniel's specific prayer, now that the seventy years were almost completed, was for God to restore "your city and your people." Daniel took God's prophecy at face value, and he understood the years of desolation as literal years that had a specific beginning and a specific ending point.

Daniel believed in the literal fulfillment of Jeremiah's prophecy of the seventy-year captivity in Babylon. God responded by giving Daniel a prophecy that announced an additional 490 years in Israel's future before the kingdom promises would be fulfilled. The time from the beginning of Jerusalem's reconstruction to the Messiah would be 483 years. But then God inserted a gap in the chronology. The death of the Messiah and another destruction of Jerusalem would take place in this gap.

God then explained to Daniel that the final seven years of Israel's prophetic future begin with a covenant. The covenant promises peace and protection for Israel, but this seven-year period of safety is cut short. "In the middle of the 'seven' he will put an end to sacrifice and offering. And on a wing of the temple he will set up an abomination that causes desolation, until the end that is decreed is poured out on him" (9:27). The last three-and-a-half years of God's prophetic timetable for Israel begins with something called "an abomination that causes desolation" that will be set up in the temple. Daniel seems to be describing specific times and events, but is that what God really intended? Again, should we interpret this as a blueprint or just a vague prediction of problems for Israel? To answer this question we need to visit with our second individual in the Bible— Jesus Christ.

Almost six centuries after Daniel made his prediction, Jesus explained its meaning to His disciples. In Matthew 24, Israel's Messiah explained what was in store for the nation. He pictured Israel's future as He detailed the events that would occur during this final seven-year period. In Matthew 24:4-14 Jesus explained to His disciples the general troubles that would occur during the first three-and-a-half years of this period. But beginning in 24:15 He focused on the specific event that would spell trouble for Israel:

> So when you see standing in the holy place "the abomination that causes desolation," spoken of through the prophet Daniel—let the reader understand—then let those who are in Judea flee to the mountains. . . . For then there will be great distress, unequaled from the beginning of the world until now—and never to be equaled again. (Matthew 24:15-16, 21)

Jesus quotes Daniel's prediction of the "abomination that causes desolation," and He makes two specific points. First, He says that Daniel's prediction was still future. Daniel's prophecy had not been fulfilled in almost 600 years, but that did not invalidate the message. It would still be fulfilled. Second, Jesus says that the event will happen exactly as Daniel predicted. Daniel's message was not some veiled description of difficult times for Israel. Daniel provided a detailed blueprint of Israel's still-future history, and the events would take place exactly as God predicted.

Though I have selected Daniel and Jesus as two specific individuals who explained to us how they interpreted earlier prophecies, they are not unique. Paul also knew these predictions of Daniel and Jesus, and he affirmed their accuracy. Paul believed the prophecies that the Antichrist would set up the "abomination that causes desolation" in the temple. "He [the Antichrist] will oppose and will exalt himself over everything that is called God or is worshiped, so that he sets himself up in God's temple, proclaiming himself to be God" (2 Thessalonians 2:4). Paul summarized the message of Daniel 9 and Matthew 24, and he expected the desecration of the temple to occur just as Daniel and Jesus predicted.

A short time later the Apostle Peter wrote his epistle to remind his readers not to fall prey to those who doubt God's predictions:

> First of all, you must understand that in the last days scoffers will come, scoffing and following their own evil desires. They will say, "Where is this 'coming' he promised?" . . . But do not forget this one thing, dear friends: With the Lord a day is like a thousand years, and a thousand years are like a day. The Lord is not slow in keeping his promise. (2 Peter 3:3-4, 8-9)

Peter reminds his audience that God doesn't forget His promises. God will bring His predictions to pass at His own time.

Does God provide a prophetic "blueprint" for the world? Or, more accurately, does God make specific predictions that He then brings to pass? The answer of Daniel, Jesus, Paul, and Peter is yes! They all looked into the Scriptures, saw prophecies that had not yet been fulfilled, and then expected God to fulfill them exactly as He had promised. They accepted God's predictions at face value, and so should we.

Prophecies Came True as Predicted

The Bible claims to predict the future, and later Bible writers expected the predictions to come true exactly as God predicted. But is there any independent way we can verify whether these predictions did actually come true? In our secular society, the testimony of others is not enough. Much like the doubting disciple Thomas we cry out, "Unless I see the nail marks in his hands and put my finger where the nails were, and put my hand into his side, I will not believe it" (John 20:25). We want objective proof before we are willing to accept any claims made by others.

Do we have any independent way to decide whether God did predict the future and whether those prophecies came true? Yes, we do. The Bible itself contains hundreds of predictions that took place exactly as God predicted. We can't look at all these prophecies, but we can look at just a few to see how God fulfilled His predictions.

The Prediction

The Fulfillment

The Messiah will be born in Bethlehem.

"But you, Bethlehem Ephrathah, though you are small among the clans of Judah, out of you will come for me one who will be ruler over Israel, whose origins are from of old, from ancient times." (Micah 5:2)

"So Joseph also went up from the town of Nazareth in Galilee to Judea, to Bethlehem the town of David, because he belonged to the house and line of David. . . . While they were there, the time came for the baby to be born." (Luke 2:4, 6)

The Messiah will ride into Jerusalem on a colt.

"Rejoice greatly, O Daughter of Zion! Shout, Daughter of Jerusalem! See, your king comes to you, righteous and having salvation, gentle and riding on a donkey, on a colt, the foal of a donkey." (Zechariah 9:9)

"As they approached Jerusalem and came to Bethphage on the Mount of Olives, Jesus sent two disciples, saying to them, 'Go to the village ahead of you, and at once you will find a donkey tied there, with her colt by her. Untie them and bring them to me. . . . This took place to fulfill what was spoken through the prophet." (Matthew 21:1-2, 4)

The Messiah will be abused.

"He was despised and rejected by men, a man of sorrows, and familiar with suffering. Like one from whom men hide their faces he was despised, and we esteemed him not." (Isaiah 53:3)

"Dogs have surrounded me; a band of evil men has encircled me, they have pierced my hands and my feet." (Psalm 22:16)

"They stripped him and put a scarlet robe on him, and then twisted together a crown of thorns and set it on his head. They put a staff in his right hand and knelt in front of him and mocked him. 'Hail, king of the Jews!' they said. They spit on him, and took the staff and struck him on the head again and again. After they

The Prediction	The Fulfillment

and mocked him, they took
off the robe and put his own
clothes on him. Then they led
him away to crucify him."
(Matthew 27: 28-31)

The Messiah's clothing will be taken and divided up.

"They divide my garments
among them and cast lots for
my clothing." (Psalm 22:18)

"When they had crucified him,
they divided up his clothes by
casting lots."
(Matthew 27:35)

The Messiah will be mocked by those who put Him to death.

"All who see me mock me; they
hurl insults, shaking their heads:
'He trusts in the LORD, let the
LORD rescue him. Let him
deliver him, since he delights in
him.' " (Psalm 22:7-8)

"Those who passed by hurled
insults at him, shaking their heads
and saying, 'You who are going to
destroy the temple and build it in
three days, save yourself! Come
down from the cross, if you are
the Son of God!' In the same way
the chief priests, the teachers of
the law and the elders mocked
him. 'He saved others,' they said,
'but he can't save himself! . . . He
trusts in God. Let God rescue him
now if he wants him.'" (Matthew
27:39-43)

The Messiah will be put to death.

"But he was pierced for our
transgressions, he was crushed
for our iniquities; the punishment that brought us peace was
upon him, and by his wounds
we are healed. We all, like

"And when Jesus had cried out
again in a loud voice, he gave up
his spirit. At that moment the curtain of the temple was torn in two
from top to bottom. The earth
shook and the rocks split." (Mat-

The Prediction	The Fulfillment

sheep, have gone astray, each of us has turned to his own way; and the LORD has laid on him the iniquity of us all. . . . For he was cut off from the land of the living; for the transgression of my people he was stricken." (Isaiah 53:5-6, 8)

The Messiah will be buried in a rich man's tomb.

"He was assigned a grave with the wicked, and with the rich in his death, though he had done no violence, nor was any deceit in his mouth." (Isaiah 53:9)	"As evening approached, there came a rich man from Arimathea, named Joseph, who had himself become a disciple of Jesus. . . . Joseph took the body, wrapped it in a clean linen cloth, and placed it in his own new tomb that he had cut out of the rock." (Matthew 27:57, 59-60)

The Messiah will rise from the dead.

"Therefore my heart is glad and my tongue rejoices; my body also will rest secure, because you will not abandon me to the grave, nor will you let your Holy One see decay." (Psalm 16:9-10)	"The angel said to the women, 'Do not be afraid, for I know that you are looking for Jesus, who was crucified. He is not here; he has risen, just as he said. Come and see the place where he lay.'" (Matthew 28:5-6)
"Yet it was the LORD's will to crush him and cause him to suffer, and though the LORD makes his life a guilt offering, he will see his offspring and prolong his days, and the will of	[Peter quotes Psalm 16 and then explains this psalm of David.] "Brothers, I can tell you confidently that the patriarch David died and was buried, and his tomb is here to this day. But he

The Prediction

the LORD will prosper in his
hand." (Isaiah 53:10)

The Fulfillment

was a prophet and knew that
God had promised him on
oath that he would place one
of his descendants on his
throne. Seeing what was
ahead, he spoke of the resurrection of the Christ, that he
was not abandoned to the
grave, nor did his body see
decay." (Acts 2:29-31)

The opposing lawyers have presented their closing
arguments to the jury. The judge turns in his chair and
presents his charge. "Men and women of the jury,
your task is to examine everything that has been presented and to arrive at a conclusion based on the
weight of evidence." You shuffle off to the jury room
to begin your deliberations. The question before you
today is this: Does God really predict the future?

God spoke on His own behalf and claimed to predict "what is yet to come" (Isaiah 44:7). Daniel, Jesus,
Paul, and Peter appeared as character witnesses to confirm God's ability to predict the future. The evidence
from history seems to bear out their testimony. Time
and again God made specific predictions in the Old
Testament. Each event occurred exactly as God had
predicted. Based on the evidence, what verdict should
you reach? "[God] has predicted multitudes of events
to happen in the future. They have come true exactly
as predicted, even though in some cases thousands of
years were involved for the fulfillment. God has

proven that He is our supernatural God with all wisdom. We have no alternative but to believe."[3]

Understanding of Prophecy Will Increase

The Bible does predict the future, but one major stumbling block for some seems to be the multitude of different interpretations for end-time events. If God's predictions are so clear, why are there so many different explanations? Why don't all Christians agree on the specifics of Bible prophecy?

We need to put this question in its proper perspective. Christians disagree about many issues in the Bible, not just prophecy. If unanimity were the criteria for establishing truth, we would all be echoing the words of Pontius Pilate: "What is truth?" Disagreements should drive us toward the Bible, not away from it. The church needs more members with the character of the ancient Bereans. "Now the Bereans were of more noble character than the Thessalonians, for they received the message with great eagerness and examined the Scriptures every day to see if what Paul said was true" (Acts 17:11).

Our desire is to understand the truth of God. But even with that desire, we still find sincere Christians who disagree on what God has said about the future. Why are there such differences? Three specific reasons surface.

First, people disagree about end-time events because no one individual has a grasp of all God's truth. Each Christian must realize that he or she still has much to learn about God's Word. I have found that disagreements arise because some Christians have

not studied a particular subject in detail. At other
times disagreements arise because people make
assumptions about what God will do in the end times,
even if the Bible is silent on that subject. Disagreements are often the result of our lack of understanding. The fault is ours, not God's.

Second, people disagree about end-time events
because of our inability to accept at face value predictions that don't match what we see in the world today.
Just over fifty years ago the prophecies about Israel
seemed so remote. The nation of Israel had not existed
for nearly 2,000 years, yet God seemed to say He had
a future for Israel. God's Word did not conform to our
perception of reality, so we had trouble accepting
God's Word. Since 1948 it has been easier for us to
understand God's predictions about Israel because the
nation is back in existence. Was the problem God's
Word, or was it our inability to trust what God had
said?

The problem with predictive prophecy is never
God's Word. Instead it is our unwillingness to acknowledge the clear meaning of God's predictions
when those prophecies, if taken at face value, seem
impossible. God's prophecies about Babylon are
clear, but few seriously thought that a literal Babylon
could play a role in the final days. We rejected the
clear meaning of God's Word because it did not
square with our understanding of current events in the
Middle East. Only when Saddam Hussein invaded
Kuwait and threatened to control the world's supply
of oil did we see how God's Word could actually

come true just as God predicted. What changed—
God's Word or our understanding of world events?

Third, people disagree about end-time events
because God predicted that His Word would not
always become clear until the events themselves were
very near. The Old Testament prophets who predicted
the first coming of Israel's Messiah did not fully understand the meaning of their words.

> Concerning this salvation, the prophets, who
> spoke of the grace that was to come to you,
> searched intently and with the greatest care, try-
> ing to find out the time and circumstances to
> which the Spirit of Christ in them was pointing
> when he predicted the sufferings of Christ and
> the glories that would follow. (1 Peter 1:10-11)

I can almost picture Isaiah and Micah having lunch
together somewhere in Jerusalem. As one prophet
reads his latest revelation from God, the other
scratches his head, trying to put the pieces of the puzzle together. They saw images of the Messiah being
born in Bethlehem, suffering for the sins of the world,
dying and coming back to life, and ruling over the
final kingdom of Israel. But they could not work out
all the details. Only as the events arrived did all the
pieces finally come together.

God announced the same truth to Daniel. After having Daniel record all his visions, God said to him,
"But you, Daniel, close up and seal the words of the
scroll until the time of the end. Many will go here and
there to increase knowledge" (Daniel 12:4). Daniel's

scroll could be read, but for most readers it remained a "closed book." The words gave a message of hope to the Jews living in the "times of the Gentiles," but the Jews did not fully understand the specific meaning of God's prophecies. Only as the time for the events drew closer would the meaning become clearer. This is what God meant when He said that "many will go here and there to increase knowledge." God was not predicting an increase in transportation—they were going "here and there" in the Bible, not in automobiles, trains, or planes!

As the "time of the end" draws closer, we should expect to see our understanding of Bible prophecy increase. World events will finally begin to line up more precisely with events predicted in the Bible. When the morning newspaper and the evening news start sounding more like the words of Daniel, Jesus, or the Apostle John, our "prophetic blinders" will be removed. God does predict the future, and His prophecies will all begin to make sense to us when world events parallel the predictions found in the Bible.

CHAPTER SEVENTEEN
WHY SHOULD I STUDY BIBLE PROPHECY?

I sat in the college mathematics class with my head
propped on my left arm. The pen in my right hand
retraced the lines and shapes I had drawn around the
margins of my paper. My goal that day was simply to
stay awake. We were one week into an introductory
section on bookkeeping, and I was incredibly bored.
Of what possible value were credits and debits to me?
I wasn't going into accounting. I planned to enter the
ministry, and I was going to Dallas Seminary. The
material on bookkeeping and accounting lacked practical relevance to my life.

I now thank God for that introduction to bookkeeping! No one ever told me that the ministry would
require skills in preparing and managing budgets or
maintaining spreadsheets. The material that seemed so
irrelevant twenty years ago has proven its importance
for my work over the past decade.

"Relevance" is a major obstacle to effective teaching. Unless I can show the relevance and practical
value of what I am teaching, many will not become
interested enough to learn. While our ideal might be

"knowledge for knowledge's sake," we filter out large amounts of information that assault our senses every day. We only allow in information that seems to have a direct bearing on our lives.

You might drive past thousands of cars every day on your way to work, and you scarcely notice them. But buy a new car and watch what happens. Suddenly you see automobiles like yours all over the highway. Did these cars magically appear the moment you purchased your new car? No, but with your new purchase that particular car model has become important to you. It has become "relevant," and you begin to notice other drivers who have bought the same car.

For many individuals Bible prophecy is also irrelevant. "Even if God predicted the future," they say, "how does that affect my life today?" Why study about events that will happen after God removes the church from the earth? If end-time events will not take place while I'm living here on earth, why should I care what God does once I'm gone? Is there any practical value for me today in studying Bible prophecy, or am I only filling my head with useless information?

God gave prophecy to change our hearts, not to fill our heads with knowledge. God never predicted future events just to satisfy our curiosity about the future. Every time God announces events that are still future, He includes with His predictions practical applications to life. God's pronouncements about the future carry with them specific advice for the "here and now." Let's look at four examples of how God expects prophecy to make a difference in our lives today.

Prophecy Produces Praise

In Romans 9–11 the Apostle Paul explains God's future program for Israel. Israel rejected God's promised blessings, and God used their rejection to bring blessing to the Gentiles through the church. The Gentiles (pictured as a "wild olive shoot") replaced Israel (the "branches" that "have been broken off") in the place of blessing (Romans 11:17). But Paul then explains that God will again restore Israel: "Israel has experienced a hardening in part until the full number of the Gentiles has come in. And so all Israel will be saved" (11:25-26).

When will Israel be restored nationally? Paul uses Isaiah 59 to show that it will happen when "the deliverer will come from Zion" (Romans 11:26, summarizing Isaiah 59:20). Both Isaiah and Paul expected God's promises to Israel to be fulfilled following the second coming of Jesus to earth. But Paul's readers in Rome would be gone before God again grafted Israel back into the place of blessing. So what relevance does this prophecy have to those Romans who read Paul's words—or to us?

After describing how God would restore Israel, Paul launched into a song of praise to God: "Oh, the depth of the riches of the wisdom and knowledge of God! How unsearchable his judgments, and his paths beyond tracing out!" (Romans 11:33). The realization that God controlled the future forced Paul to his knees in praise. A true understanding of God's program for the future gives us insight into the wisdom, knowledge, and power of the God of the universe. Prophecy not only points us toward the future, it also points us toward the majesty of God who controls the future.

Prophecy Produces Encouragement

Paul penned his first letter to the church in Thessalonica after a riot forced him from the city (Acts 17:1-9). Paul had spent only a few weeks founding the church in Thessalonica, but he must have taught them much about end-time events. Both 1 and 2 Thessalonians contain much information on the coming of Jesus and other end-time events. In 1 Thessalonians every chapter ends by pointing to the coming of Jesus.

Several events that took place after Paul left Thessalonica troubled the new church. Some members of the church had died, and their loved ones wondered if they would see them again. Those still alive had to face continued persecution. The rabble-rousers who had opposed Paul elsewhere wanted to stamp out this new work in Thessalonica. The days were so difficult that some believers wondered if the final seven-year time of trouble had come. Evidently Paul had told them about "the day of the Lord," when God would pour out His judgment on the earth. Had they entered this Tribulation period?

Paul wrote to this fledgling church and gave them God's prophetic insight into the future. In 1 Thessalonians 4:13-18 Paul explained what would happen to those Christians who had died:

> For the Lord himself will come down from heaven, with a loud command, with the voice of the archangel and with the trumpet call of God,

and the dead in Christ will rise first. After that,
we who are still alive and are left will be caught
up together with them in the clouds to meet the
Lord in the air. And so we will be with the Lord
forever. (1 Thessalonians 4:16-17)

Paul predicted that Jesus would return in the air to
gather up those Christians who had already died as
well as those who were still alive. He would then take
them all to heaven.

In the next chapter Paul explained to the Thessalonians that they would not be on earth during the coming
"day of the Lord":

While people are saying, "Peace and safety,"
destruction will come on them suddenly, as labor
pains on a pregnant woman, and they will not
escape. But you, brothers, are not in darkness so
that this day should surprise you like a thief. . . .
For God did not appoint us to suffer wrath but to
receive salvation through our Lord Jesus Christ.
(1 Thessalonians 5:3-4, 9)

The day of the Lord was still coming, but it would surprise those in spiritual darkness. The believers of Thessalonica were now "sons of the light" and would not
be part of the coming day of wrath.

Paul provides the Thessalonians with prophetic
truth about the future. He describes to them the coming time of trouble that will overtake the earth. He
also explains that God will remove the church from
the earth before that time of trouble. But God did not

give this information just to fill their heads. After each prophetic section Paul writes, "Therefore encourage each other with these words" (4:18) and "Therefore encourage one another and build each other up" (5:11). God gave this revelation to make a change in their lives.

Knowledge of the future ought to bring encouragement to those who have put their trust in Jesus. We might be experiencing difficulties now, but we know from prophecy that God is in control of the universe. He has a plan for the universe, and He has a plan for us. Knowing that God has already secured our eternal destiny can give us encouragement to face our present trials.

Prophecy Produces Stability

Paul wrote a second letter to the church in Thessalonica because questions were still being raised over their continued persecution. Evidently someone circulated a bogus letter, supposedly from Paul, stating that the end times had now arrived. "Concerning the coming of our Lord Jesus Christ and our being gathered to him, we ask you, brothers, not to become easily unsettled or alarmed by some prophecy, report or letter supposed to have come from us, saying that the day of the Lord has already come" (2 Thessalonians 2:1-2).

Paul reminds the Thessalonians of his clear teaching during the weeks he had stayed in Thessalonica: "Don't you remember that when I was with you I used to tell you these things?" (2:5). Paul summarizes the "things" he had told them earlier. In verses 3-4 he explains the appearance and activity of the "man of

lawlessness" who will go into the temple and proclaim himself to be God. In verses 6-12 Paul describes
the spiritual struggles that will take place once God
removes His restraint of evil. He notes the "signs and
wonders" Satan will use to trick the world. He shows
that these events will continue until Jesus returns to
earth and destroys this "man of lawlessness."

Having described the time of trouble coming on the
earth, Paul reminds his readers that they share a different destiny: "But we ought always to thank God for
you, brothers loved by the Lord, because from the
beginning God chose you to be saved through the
sanctifying work of the Spirit and through belief in the
truth" (2:13). Paul gently reminds his readers that they
are not in the day of the Lord because that day comes
on an unsuspecting and unbelieving world. Those
who have put their trust in Jesus share a different destiny. The Thessalonians might be suffering persecution, but that persecution is not the end-time trouble
coming on the world.

Paul must have taken much time during his stay in
Thessalonica to describe the end times and the work
of this one we call the Antichrist. But why go into
such detail if the church will not be part of that time of
trouble? Paul explains the whole program of God to
give these believers stability in uncertain times. He
begins by asking them "not to become easily unsettled
or alarmed" (2:2). He expects their knowledge of
future events to keep them from falling prey to panic.
"Don't let anyone deceive you in any way" (2:3). Paul
concludes the section by reaffirming the practical
value of prophecy for evaluating circumstances: "So

then, brothers, stand firm and hold to the teachings we passed on to you, whether by word of mouth or by letter" (2:15).

As 1991 began, the world nervously watched events in the Middle East. Would Saddam Hussein start World War III? Would he use chemical weapons? Did he have nuclear weapons? Would the Soviet Union come to his aid and launch a surprise attack against the Allied forces? Would the battle escalate into a nuclear confrontation that would destroy the earth? The world had no idea how the battle would go, and people made any number of dramatic predictions. But those who know what the Bible says about the future did not need to panic. God has a plan for the world, and the world will not end in some "accidental" nuclear holocaust.

Understanding God's plan provides stability in these difficult days. In effect, God has provided us with a basic road map of future events. We do not know everything that will take place in the future, but we do know enough to identify the major events and actors in God's end-time drama. And what we know is enough to keep our lives from spinning out of control.

Prophecy Produces Holiness

The Apostle Peter also talked about future things. In 2 Peter 3 he asked his readers "to recall the words spoken in the past by the holy prophets and the command given by our Lord and Savior through your apostles" (2 Peter 3:2). What words does he want them to recall? Beginning in verse 3 Peter describes "the last

days," which he also identifies as "the day of the
Lord." Peter reminds his readers of the end-time
prophecies still to be fulfilled.

Peter explains to his readers that God's end-time
program will come, even if the prophecies were made
thousands of years earlier. But why has God seemed
to delay fulfilling His predictions? "The Lord is not
slow in keeping his promise, as some understand slow-
ness. He is patient with you, not wanting anyone to
perish, but everyone to come to repentance" (3:9).
The end-time events have not yet come because God
wants to give everyone the opportunity to accept Jesus
Christ as their personal Savior.

God is patient, but His patience will not stop His
final plans for this sinful and corrupt world. Peter
leaps ahead in time to the "final" end of the planet we
call home: "The heavens will disappear with a roar;
the elements will be destroyed by fire, and the earth
and everything in it will be laid bare" (3:10). God will
finally destroy this present world just after His final
judgment of humanity at the great white throne (Revelation 20:11-15). What will replace this present universe? God will create "a new heaven and a new
earth, the home of righteousness" (2 Peter 3:13).

Why did Peter go into such detail describing events
that will not occur until the very end of time? What
practical application did this truth have for his readers? Peter explains the practicality of his predictions
three separate times in the passages. Each time he
links the certainty of future events with the expected
application in the present. Knowledge of the future
should affect our lives today.

Peter makes his first application in 3:11-12: "Since everything will be destroyed in this way, what kind of people ought you to be? You ought to live holy and godly lives as you look forward to the day of God and speed its coming." Prophecy should produce personal holiness. God tells us that He will judge the world and that we will appear before the judgment seat of Christ (2 Corinthians 5:10). He also tells us that everything in this world will be destroyed. Knowing what will take place helps us keep the proper perspective today.

In college and graduate school I had several professors who loved to give "pop quizzes." Anytime in the semester you could walk into class and hear those dreaded words, "Take out a sheet of paper and write your name at the top." Why do some teachers like to give pop quizzes? They have found through experience that many students will not keep up with the required class work and reading unless they know they might be held accountable at any time.

God announced through Peter that His final "pop quiz" was coming and that the grade held eternal significance. Those who never had the opportunity to hear the message of salvation or to place their trust in Christ would suffer eternal judgment. Christians who put their pleasures above their service for Christ also would see their works exposed and judged. Knowing that a day of reckoning was coming motivated Peter's audience to live holy lives and to share the gospel with those who had not yet heard.

In Peter's second application he again emphasizes this call to holiness: "So then, dear friends, since you

are looking forward to this, make every effort to be
found spotless, blameless and at peace with him"
(3:14). Knowledge of the future should result in
changes today. A bride who knows that her wedding
day is next month does not wait until the final day to
begin making preparations. The certainty of the coming day guides her in her plans and activities so she
will be prepared when the day finally arrives. God
gave us knowledge of the future so that we also would
begin preparing for it today.

Peter's final application to his audience comes in
2 Peter 3:17: "Therefore, dear friends, since you
already know this, be on your guard so that you may
not be carried away by the error of lawless men and
fall from your secure position." Again, a knowledge
of the future will keep us from error and deceit today.
Do you believe that God is working in the world
today to bring about the events He has predicted? The
true test of how firmly you believe will not be what
you say but how you live.

Why study Bible prophecy? Is our goal to produce charts and graphs and to fill our heads with
facts? If so, we are not using Bible prophecy the
way God intended. God did share with us what will
happen in the future, but He did so to change our
lives. We ought to respond to prophecy with a
sense of awe and wonder at the God of the universe
who can announce what will take place and then
bring it to pass. We ought to feel a sense of comfort
and encouragement as we realize that the God who
can work out the fate of nations also can work out
the details of our lives. This should produce stabil-

ity and maturity as we refuse to get upset by the circumstances in which we find ourselves. Finally, knowing what God is going to do should motivate us to live holy lives because someday we will stand before Him to give account.

CHAPTER EIGHTEEN
SO WHAT?

The sun slipped lower in the sky as our group
climbed to the top of a hill overlooking the Judean
wilderness. Serpentine shadows snaked through val-
leys highlighting the gnarled, twisting ravines that
claw their way toward the hills of Judah. A cool,
dry breeze whistled through the rocky gorges whispering to the shadows and calling them from their
place of hiding. The chalky hills, baked white in
the harsh light of midday, softened to a golden
bronze as they caught the last rays of sunlight.
Rocks and stones covered the hills that otherwise
seemed empty and lifeless.

As we sat silently looking over these hills in the
land of Israel, our guide pulled out a tape recorder and
turned it on. The strains of Handel's *Messiah* floated
over the hills. "Comfort ye, comfort ye my people,
saith your God. Speak ye comfortably to Jerusalem,
and cry unto her, that her warfare is accomplished,
that her iniquity is pardoned." The words, from Isaiah
40:1, were penned by the prophet seven centuries
before the coming of Israel's Messiah. God predicted

that Israel's Messiah would come to bring peace. But when would the Messiah arrive?

Isaiah announced when God's program would begin, and Handel echoed in song the event that would signal the beginning of Israel's redemption. "The voice of him that crieth in the wilderness, Prepare ye the way of the Lord, make straight in the desert a highway for our God. Every valley shall be exalted, and every mountain and hill made low, the crooked straight, and the rough places plain." Now, gazing over the Judean wilderness, I understood what Isaiah had predicted.

God promised to do the impossible for Israel. He would come to save His people, and nothing would stand in His way. Even the perpetual obstacles in the Judean wilderness could not block God's coming. Neither mountain nor valley nor twisted, crooked places would hinder Him. But when would God's program begin? It would start with "the voice in the wilderness."

Seven centuries after Isaiah made his prediction, "John the Baptist came, preaching in the Desert of Judea" (Matthew 3:1). Looking over this desolate region, I could almost hear John's voice mingling with the wind that would have carried it across the hills. John fulfilled exactly the prediction made by Isaiah. He was the voice crying in the wilderness.

We boarded our bus and began the long ascent to Jerusalem. The sky turned dark long before our bus climbed the last hill leading into the city. The members of the tour sat in silence, thinking about the truth of the words they had just heard. But as our bus topped the last hill and Jerusalem came into view, the guide played one final selection from the *Messiah*. "Hallelujah! The kingdom of this world is become the Kingdom of our Lord, and of His Christ, and He shall reign forever and ever." In just thirty minutes—the time between our stop in the Judean wilderness and our arrival in Jerusalem—we spanned the ages from the announcement of Christ's first coming to the consummation of His second coming.

Jesus came as the Lamb of God destined to take away the sin of the world, but He is coming back to earth a second time. This time He will be the lion of the tribe of Judah who will rule the nations with a rod of iron. In this book we have examined some major events that God has predicted will occur just before Jesus returns to earth.

By Way of Review

As I watch current world events and compare them to the Bible, I am amazed at how rapidly God is arranging the stage for the final act of this epic drama. Our first signpost was Israel—the nation brought back into existence after almost 1,900 years of exile among the nations. Israel is central in God's program of the ages. When Jesus comes in the air to take the church to heaven, Israel will step to the center of the stage and resume its starring role. The act begins with a signing ceremony that gives Israel her first expectation of real peace. But that peace is shattered by later events.

The Bible says much about Israel in the end times, but the prophets also named other countries in the Middle East that will be on the stage at the same time. Babylon, in modern Iraq, will rise as a leading economic power—probably through its control of oil. Iran, Libya, Sudan, and, possibly, Turkey also will play a brief part in the final days. They will launch a surprise attack against Israel that will be repulsed by God.

Some type of European confederacy will rise to fill the power vacuum left by the sudden decline of the United States. We are never told why the United States does not play a leading role in end-time events, but it doesn't. This confederation of European powers will assume the role of world peacemaker and world police officer. The ultimate leader of this coalition will claim to be God and will demand to be worshiped. When Israel refuses, he will try to wipe out the Jews. With the backing of Satan he appears to be unstoppable. Yet his end is swift and complete as Jesus casts him alive into the Lake of Fire when He finally returns to earth to assume His kingdom.

God is in the business of predicting the future. He did not make predictions like some fortune-teller at the circus just to draw a crowd. God foretold key events to establish His claim to be the only God of the universe. He offered us advice on the future so we could learn to trust Him and to live holy lives as we confidently wait for Him to bring about His plans. To the extent that the events described in this book match the exact message that God gave through His prophets, those events will take place.

Where Do You Fit In? Option 1

God gave the most dramatic and extensive prediction of future events to the Apostle John in the book of

Revelation. Beginning in chapter 4, John takes his readers on a tour of future events that dwarfs any ride found in Disney World. John describes the future time of trouble, the major participants, the return of Jesus to rule over His kingdom, the final judgment on the unsaved, and the establishment of a new heaven and a new earth with the saints of all ages living in the new Jerusalem.

But having described the future, John returns to the present in the final chapter. His closing words to his audience force us to evaluate the implications of Jesus' return for our lives. John's first point is to hammer home the fact that these events will occur as God has predicted: "The angel said to me, 'These words are trustworthy and true. The Lord, the God of the spirits of the prophets, sent his angel to show his servants the things that must soon take place'" (22:6). Jesus Christ then added His testimony to that of the angel: "Behold, I am coming soon! Blessed is he who keeps the words of the prophecy in this book" (22:7).

The words of the prophets will come to pass. Jesus will return to earth. Everything God has predicted will take place. But how do you fit into God's plan? When Jesus returns in the air for His church, will He take you with Him to heaven? Do you know without a doubt that heaven is your eternal destiny?

After testifying that the events will happen just as God predicted, John turns to his audience and offers them an opportunity to respond. He first turns to those who are not sure of their eternal destiny. They do not know if they will be inhabitants in the eternal city of Jerusalem described by John in chapter 21. John offers these readers hope: "The Spirit [the Holy Spirit of God] and the bride [the new Jerusalem, called the bride in 21:9-10] say, 'Come!' And let him who hears say, 'Come!' Whoever is thirsty, let him come; and whoever wishes, let him take the free gift of the water of life" (22:17).

Have you ever responded to God in this way? We have all done wrong and broken God's commands. In the book of Romans, Paul reminds us that "all have sinned and fall short of the glory of God" (Romans 3:23). Because everyone does wrong things, we assume that God will somehow "grade on the curve" and lower His entrance requirements for heaven. But God never lowers His standards. "For the wages of sin is death" (Romans 6:23). Only someone who is absolutely perfect (such as Jesus Christ) can ever be good enough to get into heaven through his own ability.

God wants us to be with Him for eternity. But we have sinned, and our sin must be punished. Can God provide a way to pay for our sin so we can spend eternity with Him? "But God demonstrates his own love for us in this: While we were still sinners, Christ died for us" (Romans 5:8). Jesus was perfect because He was both God and man. He lived a perfect life, and then He died on the cross. While on the cross, Jesus took on Himself the punishment for your wrongdoings.

The entrance requirements to heaven are more steep than you can afford to pay. But God Himself paid your entrance fee, and now He is standing and holding out eternity to you as a gift. That's why the Spirit and the bride say, "Come!" God has already

paid the price to purchase for you eternal life. All you
need to do is "take the free gift of the water of life."

How can you receive eternal life today? First, you
must acknowledge to God that you have sinned and
that you cannot get into heaven by your good efforts.
Second, you must believe that Jesus Christ, God's eternal Son, became a man and died on the cross to pay
for your sins. The fact that He rose from the dead
proves that His payment was sufficient. Third, you
must trust in Jesus Christ for your eternal destiny. You
must place your hope for eternal salvation in Him.
You can do this right now by praying a simple prayer
like the following:

> Dear Lord, I know that I have done wrong and
> fallen short of your perfect ways. I realize that
> my sins have separated me from you. I believe
> that you sent your Son, Jesus Christ, to earth to
> die on the cross for my sins. I put my trust in
> Jesus Christ and what He did on the cross as pay-
> ment for my sins. Please forgive me and give me
> eternal life. Amen.

If you just prayed that prayer in sincerity, then wel-
come to the family of God! God has promised that all
who put their trust in Jesus Christ as their Savior will
receive eternal life. "For God so loved the world that
he gave his one and only Son, that whoever believes
in him shall not perish but have eternal life" (John
3:16). You can depend on God.

If you did just say that prayer, let me offer some
final suggestions. First, begin reading your Bible.

Start in the New Testament in the Gospel of John to read more about the One who died to pay for your sins. Second, try to find a good church in your area where they believe and teach the Bible. A church is not a gathering place for perfect people. It is more closely akin to a hospital where hurting people can go to be mended spiritually. Tell the pastor of your decision to accept Christ, and ask him for guidance in helping you grow as a Christian.

Where Do You Fit In? Option 2

After explaining to his audience how prophecy relates to those who have not yet put their trust in Christ, John ends by sharing with those who have trusted in Christ. How should the great truths of prophecy influence believers? John gives his answer in Revelation 22:20: "He [Jesus Christ] who testifies to these things says, 'Yes, I am coming soon.'" Believers must remember that Jesus Christ is coming back to take them to be with Him in heaven. This is the next event on God's prophetic calendar. Jesus' coming in the air for His church is not to be confused with the second coming of Jesus to earth. The first event is described in 1 Thessalonians 4 and could happen at any time. The second event takes place after the coming seven-year time of trouble and will fulfill many Old Testament promises related to Israel.

Jesus reminds those who have put their trust in Him that He could come back at any time. John then speaks the words that should be on the lips of everyone who has placed his or her trust in Christ: "Amen. Come, Lord Jesus." God's words of prophecy force us to shift our gaze away from our problems toward heaven. As difficult as life might seem right now, it will not remain so forever. At any time Jesus could sound His trumpet and come to take us from this world of trouble to spend eternity with Him.

More than a century ago a Christian lawyer from Chicago experienced a tremendous time of personal difficulty. Horatio Spafford suffered a serious financial setback in the great Chicago fire. He sent his wife and children off to Europe for a time of rest while he tried to set his finances in order. On the way to England their ship was struck by another vessel and sank. Of his family only Horatio Spafford's wife escaped the disaster. All his children perished in the cold waters of the North Atlantic.

When Spafford received the telegram telling him of the tragedy, he set out at once for Europe. On the way his ship passed near the spot where the tragedy had occurred. As Spafford wrestled with his emotions of sadness, loneliness, and sorrow, he found comfort in his relationship to Christ. In the crucible of personal pain he penned the words of the song "It Is Well with My Soul."

> *When peace like a river attendeth my way,*
> *When sorrows like sea billows roll;*
> *Whatever my lot, Thou hast taught me to say,*
> *"It is well, it is well with my soul."*

I marveled at the peace that Horatio Spafford found in such trying times. But then I noticed the final verse of the song. One truth that helped Horatio Spafford stay at peace while everything around him crumbled was the truth of Christ's return. Spafford drew on the words of 1 Thessalonians 4 where the Apostle Paul announced that the Lord Himself would come down from heaven with the trumpet call of God. Spafford also quoted part of Revelation 22:20. After Jesus announced that He would come soon, the Apostle John responded, "Even so, come, Lord Jesus" (KJV). Spafford quotes the first part—"Even so"—and leaves the second part for us to fill in. And those are the very words that form the central truth of his last stanza— "Come, Lord Jesus."

Spafford did not understand why he was experiencing such personal tragedy. But he had faith in the God who promised to work "all things together for good." He knew that a day was coming when God would fulfill His promises to make all things right. Spafford's understanding of God's program for the future allowed him to trust God in the tough times he was facing.

My prayer for you is that you, too, will not be afraid to face the future. I hope that this study of prophecy gives you confidence in the God who controls history. May our words match those of Horatio Spafford.

> *And, Lord, haste the day when the faith*
> *shall be sight,*
> *The clouds be rolled back as a scroll,*
> *The trump shall resound and the Lord*
> *shall descend,*
> *"Even so"—it is well with my soul.*

NOTES

INTRODUCTION

1. *The Dallas Morning News,* 27 Nov. 1991.
2. Henry A. Kissinger, "Dealing with a New Russia," *Newsweek,* 2 Sept. 1991, p. 64.

CHAPTER 3

1. In Ezekiel 3:15 the prophet says he "came to the exiles at Tel Abib." Though the English spellings are different, the modern city of Tel Aviv in Israel and the ancient village of Tel Abib in Babylon are spelled identically in Hebrew.
2. "Airlift Rescuing Ethiopian Jews," *Chicago Tribune,* 26 May 1991, p. C3.
3. *Ibid.*
4. The best detailed explanation of this remarkable prophecy is found in *Chronological Aspects of the Life of Christ* by Harold A. Hoehner (Grand Rapids, Mich.: Zondervan, 1977), pp. 115–139.

CHAPTER 4

1. Reported by Larry Collins and Dominique Lapierre in *O Jerusalem* (London: Grafton Books, 1982), p. 348.
2. David Dolan, *Holy War for the Promised Land* (Nashville: Thomas Nelson, 1991), p. 235.

CHAPTER 5

1. Richard N. Ostling, "Time for a New Temple?" *Time,* 16 Oct. 1989, p. 64.

2. From the booklet *Treasures of the Temple* (Jerusalem: Temple Institute).
3. Asher Kaufman, "Reconstructing," *Biblical Archaeology Review* 9 (Mar./Apr. 1983): pp. 40–59.
4. Leen Ritmeyer, "Locating the Original Temple Mount," *Biblical Archaeology Review* 18 (Mar./Apr. 1992): pp. 24–45.

CHAPTER 7

1. Serge Schmemann, "Soviet Union Breathes Its Last," *The Dallas Morning News,* 26 Dec. 1991, p. 1A.
2. Marvin Cetron and Owen Davies, *Crystal Globe: The Haves and the Have-Nots of the New World Order* (New York: St. Martin's Press, 1991), p. 4.
3. Alexander King and Bertrand Schneider, *The First Global Revolution: A Report by the Council of the Club of Rome* (New York: Pantheon Books, 1991), p. 100.
4. Tom Post with Karen Breslau, "When Neo-Nazis Run Free," *Newsweek,* 29 July 1991, p. 34.
5. Karen Breslau, "Screening Out the Dark Past," *Newsweek,* 3 Feb. 1992, p. 30.
6. King and Schneider, *Global Revolution,* p. 128.
7. Allen Paul Ross, *The Table of Nations in Genesis* (Th.D. diss., Dallas Theological Seminary, 1976), p. 203.
8. *Ibid.,* p. 205.
9. Umberto Cassuto, *A Commentary on the Book of Genesis, Part II: From Noah to Abraham* (Jerusalem: Magnes Press, 1964), p. 192.

CHAPTER 8

1. King and Schneider, *Global Revolution,* p. 156.
2. *Ibid.,* p. 53.

CHAPTER 9

1. Pierre Salinger and Eric Laurent, *Secret Dossier: The Hidden Agenda behind the Gulf War,* trans. by Howard Curtis (New York: Penguin Books, 1991), pp. 223–224.

2. Kim A. Lawton, "Middle East Update: Tested by Fire," *Christianity Today,* 10 Feb. 1992, pp. 56–57.
3. David Lamb, "The Line in the Sand," *Los Angeles Times,* 25 Nov. 1990, p. 4T.
4. Aileen Vincent-Barwood, "Columbus: What If?" *Aramco World* 43 (Jan./Feb. 1992): p. 5.
5. *Ibid.,* p. 8.

CHAPTER 10

1. Jeff Levine, "How Much Time Left on Hussein's Political Clock?" *Los Angeles Times,* 3 Mar. 1991, p. 2M.
2. Robertson took this view when he wrote, "In either case the meaning is the same, that the name Babylon is to be interpreted mystically or spiritually (cf. *pneymatikos,* 11:8) for Rome." Archibald Thomas Robertson, *Word Pictures in the New Testament,* 6 vols., volume 6: *The General Epistles and the Revelation of John* (Nashville. Broadman Press, 1933), p. 430.
3. Robert H. Mounce, *The Book of Revelation* (Grand Rapids, Mich.: Eerdmans, 1977), pp. 313–314. Mounce writes, "There is little doubt that a first-century reader would understand this reference in any way other than as a reference to Rome, the city built upon seven hills."
4. Ferrel Jenkins, *The Old Testament in the Book of Revelation* (Grand Rapids, Mich.: Baker, 1976), p. 22.
5. George E. Ladd, *A Commentary on the Revelation of John* (Grand Rapids, Mich.: Eerdmans, 1972), p. 229.
6. Paul Lewis, "Dollars Can Still Get You Scotch and Waterford Crystal in Baghdad," *New York Times,* 12 May 1991, p. 10.
7. Dore Gold, "Saddam vs. a Diminished U.S. Presence," *The Jerusalem Post International Edition,* 23 Jan. 1993, p. 9.
8. Christopher Dickey, "War, Rebuilding, More War," *Newsweek,* 1 Feb. 1993, p. 48.

CHAPTER 11

1. Samir al-Khalil, *Republic of Fear: The Inside Story of Saddam's Iraq* (New York: Pantheon Books, 1989), p. x.
2. Tom Masland, "The Threat That Gets Overlooked: Iran," *Newsweek*, 25 Jan. 1993, p. 43.
3. Riad Ajami, "Turkey's Meager Harvest of Gulf Promises," *Christian Science Monitor*, 8 May 1991, p. 19.
4. Roula Khalaf, "We're Sort of in the Middle," *Forbes*, 16 Sept. 1991, p. 172.
5. Tom Post, "The Great Game, Chapter Two," *Newsweek*, 3 Feb. 1992, p. 28.
6. "Iran Bought Soviet Nuclear Weapons, Report Says," *The Dallas Morning News*, 24 Jan. 1992, p. 13A.
7. "Iran's Growing Ties to Sudan Raise Concern," *The Dallas Morning News*, 14 Dec. 1991, p. 24A.

PART THREE

1. Cetron and Davies, *Crystal Globe*, p. 17.

CHAPTER 12

1. King and Schneider, *Global Revolution*, p. 11.
2. *Ibid.*, p. 83.
3. Charles Lane and Karen Breslau, "The New Superpower," *Newsweek*, 26 Feb. 1990, p. 18.
4. "Germany's Furies," *Newsweek*, 7 Dec. 1992, p. 30.
5. *Ibid.*, pp. 30-31.
6. Josephus, *Antiquities of the Jews* 10.10.4.

CHAPTER 13

1. King and Schneider, *Global Revolution*, p. 127.

CHAPTER 14

1. Cetron and Davies, *Crystal Globe*, p. 314.
2. *Ibid.*, p. 316.

CHAPTER 15

1. James B. Pritchard, ed., *Ancient Near Eastern Texts Relating to the Old Testament,* 3d ed. (Princeton, N.J.: Princeton University Press, 1969), p. 235.

CHAPTER 18

1. T. Miles Bennett, "Interpreting Old Testament Prophecy," *Southwestern Journal of Theology* 16 (Spring 1974): p. 72.
2. Pritchard, *Ancient Near Eastern Texts,* p. 288.
3. Josh McDowell, *Evidence That Demands a Verdict* (Arrowhead Springs, Calif.: Campus Crusade for Christ, 1972), p. 332.

SCRIPTURE INDEX